Contents

Acknowledgement

Cover: cartoon, 'Manager Peel Taking His Farewell Benefit', *Punch*, 11 July 1846.

SEMINAR STUDIES IN HISTORY

General Editor: Roger Lockyer

Peel and the Conservative Party 1830–1850

Paul Adelman

LONGMAN
London and New York

Longman Group UK Limited,
Longman House, Burnt Mill, Harlow,
Essex CM20 2JE, England
and Associated Companies throughout the world.

Published in the United States of America
by Longman Inc., New York.

First published 1989
Fifth impression 1993

Set in 10/11 point Baskerville (Linotron)
Printed in Malaysia by CL

ISBN 0 582 35557 5

British Library Cataloguing in Publication Data
Adelman, Paul.
   Peel and the Conservative Party 1830–1850.
   – (Seminar studies in history).
   1. Great Britain. Peel, Sir Robert, 1788–
1850 II. Series
941.081'092'4

   ISBN 0-582-35557-5

Library of Congress Cataloging-in-Publication Data
Adelman, Paul.
   Peel and the Conservative Party, 1830–1850 / Paul Adelman.
     p. cm. – (Seminar studies in history)
   Bibliography: p.
   Includes index.
   ISBN 0-582-35557-5 : £3.25
   1. Peel, Robert, Sir, 1788–1850. 2. Conservative Party (Great
Britain) – History. 3. Conservatism – Great Britain – History – 19th
century. 4. Great Britain – Politics and government – 1837–1901.
5. Great Britain – Politics and government – 1830–1837. I. Title.
II. Series.
DA536.P3A54 1989
941.081'092'4–dc19
      88-38407
      CIP

Seminar Studies in History

Founding Editor: Patrick Richardson

Introduction

The Seminar Studies series was conceived by Patrick Richardson, whose experience of teaching history persuaded him of the need for something more substantial than a textbook chapter but less formidable than the specialised full-length academic work. He was also convinced that such studies, although limited in length, should provide an up-to-date authoritative introduction to the topic under discussion as well as a selection of relevant documents and a comprehensive bibliography.

Patrick Richardson died in 1979, but by that time the Seminar Studies series was firmly established, and it continues to fulfil the role he intended for it. This book, like others in the series, is therefore a living tribute to a gifted and original teacher.

Note on the System of References:

A bold number in round brackets (**5**) in the text refers the reader to the corresponding entry in the Bibliography section at the end of the book. A bold number in square brackets, preceded by 'doc.' [**doc. 6**] refers the reader to the corresponding item in the section of Documents, which follows the main text.

ROGER LOCKYER
General Editor

Foreword

Peel has been called by one recent writer 'arguably the greatest peace-time Prime Minister in British history'(**123**); another historian regards him as 'the founder of modern Conservatism' (**115**). Yet whatever Peel's achievements as a legislator and parliamentarian, or in building up and leading his party in the years following the passage of the Great Reform Bill, by the time of his death in 1850 the great Conservative Party was once again out of power and well on the way to being shattered irrevocably into two sections, divided between a minority of free-trade Peelites who had supported him unequivocally over the repeal of the Corn Laws in 1846, and the bulk of Protectionist Conservatives. For this outcome Peel bears much personal responsibility, as even disciples like Gladstone admitted. The main purpose of this short study is to analyse how and why this process took place in the years between 1830 and 1850; though to round off the story, a penultimate chapter has been added on the history of the Peelites until their merger into a new Liberal Party in 1859.

The twenty years of Peel's political domination present a fascinating and instructive period for the student of modern British history. For it raises questions which go to the very heart of our political system. Why do parties develop and what do they stand for? What part is played in their development by 'interests' and 'principles'? What is the responsibility of the party leader to his members, to the electorate and to the nation? These are problems which are still with us. This book is therefore very much a study in British political history. It concentrates on only one aspect of Peel's career, though a very important one. It is worth emphasising, therefore, that some major topics – finance and trade, Ireland, Chartism – are dealt with only from the point of view of Conservative party politics and not as subjects in their own right; and the treatment of them is inevitably foreshortened. Indeed, one important topic (British foreign policy) is almost completely ignored, since as far as the Conservative Party in the 1840s was concerned (and indeed the House of Commons) it was more or less an uncontentious subject.

Much detailed historical work has been carried out by scholars, particularly in the last thirty years or so, on Peel and the politics of his age, as indicated in the bibliography, and it is upon their research that this book is based. One name, however, may be singled out. My reliance upon and admiration for the writings of Professor Norman Gash will be evident in the pages that follow.

Paul Adelman

Part One: The Emergence of the Conservative Party

1 Peel and Toryism

Whatever view one takes of Peel's political development after 1830, his later Conservatism was firmly based on the traditions of Toryism with which he had grown up in the age of Lord Liverpool, whose long administration spanned the years between 1812 and 1827. Those traditions owed much to the inspiration of 'the immortal William Pitt' (in the phrase of a Tory pamphleteer), in whose wartime ministries after 1793 Liverpool and many of his leading colleagues, such as Eldon and Sidmouth, had served. It was during the years of Pitt's political domination until his early death in 1806, that the doctrines of a new Toryism developed, based on unflinching support for the war against France and the defence of the established constitution in Church and State, as opposed to the ideas of peace, reform and progress associated with the Foxite Whigs and Radicals (**69**). Peel's Toryism was therefore partly the result of family background. His father, though a leading cotton magnate, was a Pittite Tory; and he groomed his son for a political career as a government supporter almost from birth. The young Robert Peel was given a conventional upper-class education at Harrow and Oxford which enabled him in 1809, at the age of twenty-one, to enter the House of Commons for an Irish rotten borough purchased by his father. A year later he was appointed to a junior government post. Thereafter he held office almost continuously until 1830, notably as Irish Secretary between 1812 and 1818, and as Home Secretary between 1821 and 1827 and from 1828 to 1830.

As Irish Secretary Peel was a firm supporter of the constitutional *status quo*. He was committed to the Act of Union of 1801 which had abolished the separate Irish Parliament and made Ireland part of the legislature of the United Kingdom; but Roman Catholics, though allowed to vote, were forbidden by law to sit in the House of Commons. Peel, however, was a rigid opponent of the extension of political rights to Roman Catholics. Similarly he defended the rights and privileges which the Church of Ireland gained from its anomalous position as the established Church of the land, even though it embraced only a tiny minority of Anglicans. These views, and the vigour with which Peel dealt with the perennial problems of disorder in Ireland — the results largely of an iniquitous land-holding system and religious and racial resentments at English domination — led the great Irish nationalist leader, Daniel O'Connell, to dub him 'Orange Peel', a reference to the Irish Protestant extremist Orange Order. This was unfair; but Peel's six years in Ireland, though they made him acutely aware of the problems of combating crime and violence in society, were a largely sterile period in Anglo-Irish relations.

Peel's work as Home Secretary was more constructive. It was his well-known reforms after 1822 which gave him his greatest claim to fame during this period. There was nothing particularly original about his changes in the Criminal Code and prison administration; in both respects he was not prepared to go as far as the more enlightened reformers of the time demanded. The Metropolitan Police Act of 1829 (which was passed under Wellington's premiership, but its principles had been outlined as early as 1822) is a much greater example of Peel's acuity, statesmanship and political courage, since its introduction meant overcoming the prejudices of centuries amongst all classes of society (**80**). In so far as they were concerned with the more effective preservation of law and order, Peel's reforms represent an antidote to the clumsy measures of his predecessor, Lord Sidmouth, who was responsible for the use of spies and troops, the suspension of Habeas Corpus and, following Peterloo, the passing of the Six Acts in 1819, all to combat the outburst of popular agitation that marked the immediate post-war years [**doc. 1**]. Peel's reforms also represent an important strand in the doctrine of Toryism in the 1820s, and may not unfairly be linked with the other administrative reforms of the Liverpool government, particularly in the fields of finance and commerce.

Indeed, as chairman of the Currency Commission in 1819, Peel helped to initiate the return to the gold standard which, though deflationary, did lead eventually to a more stable price level, followed by tougher budgets which by the mid-1820s were producing revenue surpluses. This encouraged Lord Liverpool to introduce the first phase of free-trade policy, associated particularly with William Huskisson, President of the Board of Trade after 1823, and Frederick Robinson, Chancellor of the Exchequer. Huskisson was responsible also for the important Corn Law of 1828 (introduced under Wellington) which modified the notorious Act of 1815 by introducing a more flexible sliding scale. These policies had the wholehearted support of Peel (**117, 118**). They had a profound effect on his later economic thought and practice, and lead Gash to declare that 'the work of Peel's great ministry of 1841–46 . . . can only be appreciated when it is seen as a conscious resumption of the principles and policies initiated in 1819–27' (**83**).

The long years of government and administration which Peel experienced between 1812 and 1830 strengthened and confirmed a Toryism which was both temperamental and based on intellectual conviction; for the general view of Peel's political persona held by his contemporaries, with much justification, was one of coldness, caution and reserve. 'His smile was like the silver plate on a coffin', in O'Connell's notorious phrase. Anthony Ashley (Lord Shaftesbury) and the diarist, Charles Greville, used very similar language; and Disraeli, in an acute and not unsympathetic portrait, stressed his want of imagination and knowledge of human nature [**doc. 6**]. Peel remained apparently unmoved emotionally by the great social problems of his age, and (according to Gash) viewed events with 'the detachment of a rational intellect' (**80**); though this judgement has been qualified by another historian who sees a more emotional and passionate side to Peel's political nature (**118**). Peel's Toryism meant a conscientious concern with effective government and efficient administration; with making things work, with solving immediate problems rather than with fanciful schemes or Gladstonian 'great causes'. His feet were always planted firmly on the ground.

Experience taught Peel, therefore, that the essence of Toryism lay in a commitment to 'strong government': firm leadership, sound administration, the maintenance of law and order without fear or favour, the recognition of rights and duties. But what did 'strong government' seek to defend? The answer that Peel gave – 'the maintenance of our settled institutions in Church and State' – meant a reiteration of the commonplaces of the Tory creed. It accepted, for example, the rightful dominance of the landed aristocracy, particularly in politics, and therefore demanded a resolute defence of the constitutional privileges of the House of Lords. 'The question only is — what, in a certain state of public opinion, and in a certain position of society, is the most effectual way of maintaining the legitimate influence and authority of a territorial aristocracy' (**11**, iv). This doctrine might imply a measure of political flexibility; at no time did it lead to any genuine support for parliamentary reform, even though Peel was too intelligent to believe that the question could be postponed for ever (**105**).

Like all Liverpool's Cabinet, he believed that with all its faults the old parliamentary system on the whole gave political power and influence to those best fitted to exercise them, without excluding men with no great advantages of birth or wealth from the legislature and government. It provided effective, restrained and honest government. Peel might protest in 1830 when the Whigs were in power, that he had always reserved to himself 'full liberty to give the franchise to great towns on any fitting occasion' (**10**, ii); but somehow when he was a Tory minister the occasion never seemed to arise. Indeed, as his opening speech on the Reform Bill in March 1831 indicated, he had always believed that even small symbolic gestures to popular representation — the transfer of a seat to Manchester, for example — might undermine the whole fragile but venerable structure of the old parliamentary system. It was a point of view expressed perfectly by Lord Liverpool himself in 1821 in his comments on the proposed disfranchisement of the corrupt borough of Grampound [**doc. 2**]

As with the aristocracy, so with the Established Church. Support for the status of the Church of England was part of the very blood and tissue of Toryism; an outlook compounded of tradition, instinct and political necessity, given the close links that existed between the structure of the Anglican Church and the social and political *status quo*. This did not exclude internal church reform (as Peel was to show with his foundation of the Ecclesiastical Commission in 1835) or even minor concessions to the Dissenters. What it did mean, however, was that there was to be no yielding over the central issue of the rights of the Established Church and the fulfilment of its religious mission to the nation. For Peel, therefore, this implied opposition to Roman Catholic emancipation on grounds of principle; it would destroy the constitutional supremacy of the Church of England 'by law established' and undermine the position of the Crown, its Supreme Governor. Other members of Liverpool's Cabinet, however, led by George Canning, supported civil equality for Roman Catholics on opportunist grounds, because of its likely salutary effects on the perennial problems of Ireland. Since the Cabinet was so divided on the issue, it was agreed that the problem of Catholic emancipation should remain an open one. In this way a settlement was deliberately postponed until in 1828—29 the crisis in Ireland destroyed the fragile compromise (**55**).

It was Peel's Protestant convictions that led to his refusal to join the Cabinet of George Canning — together with Eldon and Wellington — following Lord Liverpool's collapse and retirement early in 1827 [**doc. 3**]. It was only when Wellington became Prime

Minister in 1828 that Peel resumed office as Home Secretary and leader of the House of Commons, virtually second-in-command in the government. But as both men soon became acutely aware, it became more and more difficult to ignore the Catholic problem. The repeal of the Test and Corporations Act in February 1828, at the instigation of the Whig aristocrat Lord John Russell, backed up by a strong Dissenters' campaign, removed a complicating factor which had always blanketed the emancipation question, and left it therefore isolated and ripe for settlement. 'It is really a gratifying thing', wrote Russell after the repeal, 'to force the enemy to give up his first line, that none but Churchmen are worthy to serve the State, and I trust we shall soon make him give up the second, that none but Protestants are' (**31**). Even more important were events in Ireland. The election of O'Connell for County Clare in the summer of 1828, as the result of a revolt by the Roman Catholic freeholders against traditional English electoral domination, was a direct challenge to Wellington's government, since as a Roman Catholic O'Connell was by law unqualified to sit in the House of Commons. To allow 'the Liberator' to take his seat in Parliament would necessitate a change in the law − in effect, Catholic emancipation; to oppose him would mean the risk of civil disorder and violence in Ireland, with the inevitable repetition in the future of further 'County Clares'. The Duke took the threat of violence seriously; and, never a doctrinaire Tory, concluded that on purely political grounds emancipation must be conceded, even if this meant browbeating the House of Lords and facing the prospect of a Tory revolt in the Commons (**86**).

To deal with the Lower House, Wellington once again needed the support of his second-in-command. In a letter to the Duke on 11 August 1828, Peel accepted the logic of his case for emancipation (he was after all an ex-Irish Secretary himself) but insisted, nevertheless, on tendering his resignation. By the New Year, however, his high-principled stand was weakening. On 12 January 1829, Peel indicated to the Prime Minister that 'if my retirement should prove ... *an insuperable obstacle*' to the passing of an Emancipation Bill, then he would be prepared to continue in office and see the measure through. The Duke responded in his famous appeal: 'I tell you frankly that I do not see the smallest chance of getting the better of these difficulties if you should not continue in office' (**10**, i). Peel therefore submitted, and agreed to shoulder the burden in the House of Commons. The Bill passed through the Commons early in 1829 as a result of Whig support (142 MPs voted against it); and the demoralised Lords subsequently passed it by a two-to-one majority in a mood of sullen resentment. The Roman Catholic Emancipation Act of 1829 was a simple one, largely due to Peel's insistence. It granted full civil rights to Roman Catholics, with a few minor reservations, and sensibly ignored the tricky problem of the status of the Roman Catholic Church in England; though, in a gesture of political spite, the franchise qualification in Ireland was raised from forty shillings to ten pounds.

The consequences of the 'constitutional revolution' of 1829 for the Tories were profound. It fragmented the party even further into 'Ultras' (right-wing Tories), liberal Tories, and followers of Wellington; and if Peel was denounced by the Ultras as a 'traitor' to his party and forced to abandon his university seat at Oxford, even the Duke was execrated by a fellow peer as 'the most unprincipled, most heartless, most artful . . . and most dangerous man that this country has seen for many a long year' (**128**). Moreover, 'Catholic Emancipation was the battering-ram that broke down the old unreformed system' (**34**). It showed what could be done, under pressure, to carry through a measure opposed initially by powerful forces in Parliament and the country; a salutary lesson for all reformers. As a consequence, the influence of both Crown and Lords was weakened – and at the behest not of Whigs or Radicals but of the Tory leaders. In addition, by removing the problem of Catholic rights once and for all from the English political scene, it brought the issue of parliamentary reform immediately and inevitably into first place on the national agenda. For this and other reasons, the Wellington government was therefore ill-prepared for the general election that followed the death of King George IV in June 1830.

That election, despite a background of public excitement, disorder and economic distress, seemed outwardly little different from its predecessors; only a quarter of the parliamentary seats, for example, were contested, and as far as the government was concerned there were no great losses or gains. Nevertheless, beneath the surface many could perceive a strong current in favour of change. 'He must be a very bold fool', wrote the aged reactionary, Eldon, to his brother, 'who does not tremble at what seems to be fast approaching' (**34**). The political situation was therefore extraordinarily confused when Parliament reassembled in November. Characteristically, however, Wellington misread the public mood. His defiant speech to the Lords in defence of the established constitution led to the government's defeat in the House of Commons by an opposition bloc of Whigs, Radicals and, in an act of political revenge, thirty or so Ultras. The Duke thereupon resigned, despite the fact that he still had the confidence of King William IV, and Earl Grey and the reformers assumed power [**doc. 4**]. This 'was in its way the end of the old personal monarchy' (**100**); and thus another Tory principle, the 'independence' of the Crown, that is, the right of the monarch, in principle, to appoint a Prime Minister who would carry on the King's government irrespective of the party composition of the House of Commons, had received what was virtually a mortal blow.

This was the end of an era; not only for the nation but for the Tory party. Peel himself was not too unhappy at the fall of the Wellington administration. He was only too conscious of the falsity of his own position as the Duke's right-hand man; damned by the Ultras for his betrayal over Catholic Emancipation, and by the liberal Tories for his desertion of Canning and support for the reactionary Wellington. After the recent gruelling crises and a long ministerial career, he was glad of a respite for rest and reflection. His political career was clearly entering a new phase. Now he had no real rival to challenge his pre-eminence in the ranks of the Opposition members in the House of Commons. As if to underline the importance of 1830 in British party history, that Opposition comes to be designated the Conservative Party; and Sir Robert Peel (as he became that year on the death of his father, the baronet) was destined to become its leader [**doc. 5**].

2   Peel in Opposition, 1830−41

Peel's Conservatism

How then did Peel's political principles change or develop after 1830? The key event for him, as for so many others, was the Great Reform Bill of 1832. Peel opposed it from the start, deliberately and vehemently. It was the extremism of the Bill that horrified him, both in its detailed provisions and in the revolutionary temper it inspired among the populace at large. In his opening attack on reform in March 1831 he did not deny some of the grosser evils of the old parliamentary system. Nevertheless, he listed its merits in the customary way of Tory apologists: dependable support for the executive; provision of places in the Commons for able young men who lacked independent means; the wide social basis of the franchise, etc; and he pointed to the obvious anomalies contained in the Whigs' franchise and redistribution proposals. But Peel was concerned above all with the wider, long-term consequences of the Bill. He believed that the Whig programme would not satisfy the forces it was designed to appease, and would thus unsettle all established habits of order and obedience and render stable government well-nigh impossible. 'When you have once established the overwhelming influence of the people over this House . . . what other authority in the State can − nay what other authority in the State ought to − control its will or reject its decisions?' (**11**, ii). It was an attitude of mind summed up in his famous simile − 'I was unwilling to open a door which I saw no prospect of being able to close' − made in the speech to the Commons of 6 July 1831 in which he presented his final case against the Reform Bill [**doc. 7**].

Peel's opposition to the Reform Bill on grounds of principle, together with his recognition of the overwhelming Commons' majority in favour of reform after the general election of 1831, meant that he was unprepared to support any compromise schemes that might emerge in the House of Lords to avoid a possible lavish creation of Whig peers to push the Reform Bill through. Nor would he countenance the even wilder schemes put about by the Ultras in the House of Commons which aimed at overthrowing the Whigs at any cost, establishing some sort of Tory-inspired government and then attempting to carry a modified measure of reform. Peel's attitude is further explained by his sensitivity to the charge of 'betrayal', as in 1829. 'He was', he told the diarist Croker, 'sick with eating pledges, and would take care to avoid them for the future' (**7**, ii). Peel described his position to his friend and colleague Goulburn:

'Resistance in the House of Commons may be fruitless, but that is no reason why the principle of the Bill should not be vigorously and decidedly opposed . . . But my intention is to be no party to any measure of Reform of Parliament brought forward distinctly as a substitute for the Bill . . . I shall consider very maturely indeed before I form a connection with the Ultra-Tory party.' (**10**, ii)

Peel was as good as his word. He refused to have any hand in the formation of a new government after the resignation of Earl Grey in April 1832 following the King's refusal to create new peers; and the Whigs therefore soon came back into power. This only added salt to the wounds which the Ultras felt they had already suffered at Peel's hands. In the end, of course, as was inevitable, the Whigs carried the substance of their Bill; and though Peel viewed its effects with grim foreboding, in a remarkable speech to the Commons in February 1833 he accepted that the reform question was 'finally and irrevocably disposed of [**doc. 9**].

Peel's rapid acceptance of parliamentary reform in 1833 as a *fait accompli* and his distancing himself from the Ultras during the reform crisis, were important for the future. If, as Gash suggests, 'substantially the foundations for the Victorian two-party system were laid by the division of politicians into Reformers and Conservatives over the Bill of 1831' (**45**), the use of the term 'Conservative' – now becoming the normal appellation for the Opposition – implied for Peel a less narrow, less dogmatic party than the Tories had been before 1830. This did not, however, mean any desertion of those fundamental political principles he had built up during his earlier ministerial career; they were to remain the bedrock of Peel's 'new' Conservatism. In a speech in 1838, he stated that

'By conservative principles I mean . . . the maintenance of the Peerage and the Monarchy – the continuance of the just powers and attributes of King, Lords and Commons in this country . . . By conservative principles I mean that, coexistent with equality of civil rights and privileges, there shall be an established religion and imperishable faith and that established religion shall maintain the doctrines of the Protestant Church . . . By conservative principles, I mean . . . the maintenance, defence and continuance of those laws, those institutions, that society, and those habits and manners, which have contributed to and mould and form the character of Englishmen.' (**3**, i)

Indeed, the need for strong government in order to 'conserve' the fundamental institutions of the country was now even more imperative, given the Whigs' massive electoral victory in 1832 and the growing power and ambitions of Radicalism, the enemy of everything the Conservative Party stood for. It would be fatal, therefore, Peel insisted, for the Opposition — now reduced to some 150 MPs — to seek sudden tactical victories in Parliament, as some were suggesting, in order to undermine and perhaps temporarily overthrow the Whig government, particularly in alliance with the Radicals. That would merely display to the country at large the Conservatives' factiousness and lack of conviction in their own principles [**doc. 8**].

In any case, Peel had argued in his great speech in February 1833 accepting the Reform Act that one of its major consequences was to render obsolete 'the old system of party tactics' (**11**, ii). Given the perils that faced the nation, it behoved the Opposition, therefore, to sustain the Whig ministry when necessary against its own Radical left-wing, until they were in a position to form a government of their own. At the moment, however, the Conservatives hardly amounted to a genuine parliamentary party, and lacked even an accepted leader: Peel did not really achieve that position until he formed his first ministry in 1834–35. What all this implied, therefore, was that Peel was prepared to judge the Whigs' legislative measures on their merits, and abjure factious opposition. Hence he strongly approved of the government's Coercion Bill for Ireland in 1833, which was denounced by the Radicals and their Irish 'tail'. He supported the new Poor Law Act in 1834 and the Municipal Corporations Act in the following year; indeed, in letters to the Duke of Wellington, he expressed his irritation at the Lords' cavilling over the latter measure. He even supported some degree of reform for the Church of Ireland; though he refused on principle to support Lord John Russell's scheme of 'lay appropriation' – the use of the displaced revenues of the Church for secular rather than religious purposes.

Sensible as these arguments might appear to Peel and his supporters, they still remained purely negative. Peel believed that the Conservatives must also adopt more positive policies if they were to work their passage back into office again. In particular, they had to widen the social basis of their support beyond their traditional associations with the Tory aristocracy, the country gentry and the Anglican clergy, into the ranks of the middle classes — 'to conciliate the goodwill of the sober-minded and well-disposed portions of the community'. As far back as 1822, in a perceptive letter to J. W. Croker, he had seen the dangers in the Tories cutting themselves off from the new social changes and currents of opinion in the nation at large. 'It seems to me', he wrote, 'a curious crisis when public opinion never had such influence on public measures, and yet never was so dissatisfied with the share which it possessed' (**7**, i). Now, under the new electoral regime, the middle classes were more important than ever; and Peel believed that a Conservative Party in opposition, acting with 'sense, firmness and moderation', could in fact offer them more than an increasingly divided and irresolute Whig Cabinet, pushed into further and further extremes by the forces of the Irish party, Dissent and radicalism. This was, *inter alia*, the message of the Tamworth Manifesto (see p. 17) of 1834. Its deliberate appeal to the new middle-class electorate was reiterated in a series of outstanding public speeches given by Peel over the next few years, notably in the City of London and Glasgow. 'We deny', Peel proclaimed at Glasgow in 1837, 'that we are separated by any line of interest, or any other line of demarcation, from the middling classes' (**81**).

What Peel seemed to be envisaging was a Conservative Party which, without denying its aristocratic links or the interests of its traditional supporters, could yet harness to its purposes the energy, influence and abilities of the new middle class. This depended, however, on the promulgation of a progressive Conservatism more in tune with their 'enlightened' opinions. Hence the famous commitment in the Tamworth Manifesto to 'the correction of proved abuses and the redress of real grievances' which, at the very least, seemed to offer Conservative support for some measure of relief for Dissenters' disabilities and for internal reform of the Anglican Church both at home and in Ireland [**doc. 11**]. What we see therefore after 1832 is the powerful espousal by Peel of a more positive and practical Conservatism which, coupled with his own outstanding abilities and experience, would gradually enable him to impose his leadership on the Conservative Party and indeed on the House of Commons itself [**doc. 10**].

Peel's 'progressivism' over tactics and policy was coupled with a constitutional doctrine which remained distinctly old-fashioned. When, following the dismissal of Melbourne by William IV he was appointed Prime Minister at the end of 1834, he claimed the right as the King's nominee to a 'fair trial' by the House of Commons, despite the fact that his party still lacked a parliamentary majority. 'I am yet still resolved', he told the House in February, 'to persevere to the last in maintaining the prerogative of the Crown and in fulfilling those duties which I owe to my king and my country' (**11**, iii). Yet even Peel realised the ultimate futility of his gesture and shortly afterwards resigned following his 'Hundred Days' in office.

Nevertheless, despite the Commons' rejection of his constitutional claim, Peel's declaration is of the first importance for an understanding of his fundamental political outlook. It meant that Peel, like the majority of the members of Liverpool's Cabinet in the 1820s, regarded himself primarily as a 'Ministerialist' in politics (**76**); that is, whether as Home Secretary or Prime Minister, he saw himself first and foremost as the 'King's Minister', owing a personal allegiance to the sovereign, and through the sovereign to the nation at large. This is a 'national' rather than a purely 'party' conception of political duty; and it is a theoretical view which was both confirmed and strengthened by his political practice in the 1830s, as witness his constant emphasis on the need for strong government and his forbearance towards the problems of the Whig ministries. In many ways, therefore, as Gash has argued in a classic article, Peel was not fundamentally a party politician (**110**); a point which he himself put eloquently when he was Prime Minister in the 1840s.

'I see it over and over again repeated, that I am under a personal obligation for holding the great office which I have the honour to occupy . . . that I was placed in that position by a party . . . I am not under an obligation to any man, or to any body of men, for being compelled to undergo the official duties and labour which I have undertaken . . . I have served four Sovereigns . . . and there was but one reward which I desired, namely, the simple acknowledgement on their part that I had been to them a loyal and faithful Minister.' (**11**, iv)

Peel was therefore a proponent of what Gash calls, 'the governmental ethic' (**110**): a parliamentary party was there to sustain a government, not to create or control it. 'A Government', he told

Wellington in 1846, 'ought to have a natural support. A Conservative Government should be supported by a Conservative Party' (**10**, iii). In Peel's political creed, then, party loyalty did not come first; and he reiterated time and time again, in an often somewhat grating way, his personal integrity and personal responsibility as chief minister of the Crown. 'If I exercise power, it shall be upon my conception — perhaps imperfect, perhaps mistaken, but my sincere conception — of public duty', he said after the general election of 1841 (**11**, ii).

These views meant that for Peel Conservatism was not to be equated solely with the Conservative Party, and certainly not with its traditional economic interests. To him the Conservative Party was primarily 'a constitutional and religious party', committed now to the defence of the electoral *status quo* and the Established Church, and it was indeed over the latter issue above all that the Whigs and Conservatives divided during most of the 1830s (**37**). Though Peel accepted and defended the protectionist creed over agriculture, he always did so on pragmatic grounds, and, in the spirit of Liverpool and Huskisson, he never regarded the defence of the Corn Laws as a *sine qua non* of Conservatism. 'I have no hesitation in saying', he proclaimed in a speech in 1839, 'that unless the existence of the Corn-law can be shown to be consistent, not only with the prosperity of agriculture and the existence of the landlords' interest, but also with the protection and the maintenance of the general interests of the country . . . the Corn-law is practically at an end' (**11**, iii). High-minded as these doctrines appear, it did mean (as recent historians have argued) that the Conservative Party of Peel's imagination was not quite the Conservative Party as it really was: a party that in the eyes of the bulk of its supporters existed to maintain the economic interests of farmers and landlords (**122**, **123**). It was a self-delusion for which Peel was to pay dearly. In the end in 1846 he was to be destroyed by the 'brute votes' of the Conservative backbenchers themselves; less clever, less rational, but also more devoted party men than the Prime Minister himself.

Conservative recovery

The years of Conservative domination in the 1840s were not anticipated, however, in 1832. 'No smash given by Napoleon in the midst of his greatest successes', wrote a leading Conservative supporter after the general election at the end of that year, 'was more complete and terrific than the overthrow which has struck our

Party to the ground' (**128**). The Opposition, which had already suffered drastic blows in the general election of 1831, was now reduced still further to a total of about 150 MPs; a beleaguered minority amid the great tide of Whigs and Radicals who swept into the House of Commons in the aftermath of reform. The election of 1832 revealed one trend at least which was to outlast this Parliament. The Conservative Party was now very much the party of England; more than a hundred of its seats were centred there. Its power had been undermined in Ireland and Scotland and to some extent in Wales; and even in England it was able to win only two seats out of the host of new boroughs created by the Reform Act. In the counties too the Conservatives did disastrously, mainly due to the fact that for a variety of reasons the newly-enfranchised tenant farmers proved to be ardent reformers.

After a generation in which the Tories had been the natural party of government, their Conservative successors had to adapt to the difficult and unpalatable task of becoming an effective Opposition; as Peel said, 'almost a contradiction in terms' (**10**, ii). This was not rendered any easier by the fact that, in the earlier 1830s, the party lacked any real unity. The Ultras were strong in the Upper House, and even the Duke of Wellington found it difficult to restrain their opposition to important Whig measures in defiance of the more cautious attitude of the party leadership. In the Commons, led by such influential members as Sir Richard Vyvyan and Sir Edward Knatchbull, the Ultras still acted as a separate group, and were intensely critical of what they regarded as Peel's lack of party zeal during the Reform crisis and its aftermath (**98**). Peel, for his part, convinced of their imprudence and irresponsibility, was determined to maintain his distance. 'I would not abandon any one opinion I entertain', he told Goulburn in 1831, 'in order to conciliate Ultra-Tory support' (**128**). Peel thus retained his freedom of action; but it left him in some ways an aloof, isolated and resentful figure within the ranks of the parliamentary party. As Mrs Arbuthnot, the Tory political hostess, wrote with pardonable exaggeration: 'As to Peel, he appears to hate everybody and everybody hates him . . . He is supercilious, haughty and arrogant . . .' (**2**, ii).

Nevertheless, the position of the Conservative Party after 1831 was not as hopeless as it seemed. The Conservative influence of the landlords was still important in the boroughs and considerable in the counties; and their power in the latter areas was likely to increase if − as later happened − the farmers became suspicious of the Whigs' devotion to agricultural protection. Similarly, the Conservative instincts of Anglicans were bound to be reinforced when the Whig governments began to lay secular hands upon the privileges and property of the Church of England. The House of Lords too remained a Tory bastion, and William IV himself was no friend of the Whigs. Moreover, the Conservatives were quicker off the mark than their opponents in strengthening their party organisation. As early as 1831, a group of leading Conservatives, led by such men as Joseph Planta, William Holmes and Sir Henry Hardinge, set up a small committee — the so-called 'Charles Street Gang' — to provide some sort of central organisation for their party. In the following year, this led to the establishment of the Carlton Club as a Conservative headquarters to deal with electoral matters. The same year saw the real beginning of the foundation of Conservative Associations throughout the country.

Above all, perhaps, the Conservatives possessed in Peel a man who in terms of intellect, experience and national influence stood head and shoulders above any other member of the party, or of the House of Commons, as even his political opponents admitted [**doc. 10**]. Whatever the reservations of some Tories, the party needed Peel; and during the early 1830s he began to develop a policy and strategy which enabled him gradually to impose his leadership on the Conservative Party and give it a greater degree of coherence and credibility. Peel was concerned during these years not with short-term tactical victories over the Whigs, but with the tasks of strengthening the Opposition party in the House of Commons and building up Conservative sentiment amongst the electors outside. This could come about, he believed, as a result of tensions and disputes within the heterogeneous mass of Reformers in the House of Commons; and, in particular, as a direct consequence of extremist measures introduced by the Whig Cabinets under Radical pressure. This would antagonise moderate opinion in the Commons and the country which had supported reform in 1831, and make it sympathetic to the Opposition. The Conservative Party would thus become 'the haven of the disenchanted' (**128**). But, as we have seen, Peel also believed that his party must make a more positive appeal to the middle classes, in order to convince them that the Conservative Party too, in its own way, could be seen as a party of reform. For the moment, therefore, Peel preached a policy of patience and realism. As he wrote to Goulburn in 1833: 'I think such a party acting with firmness and restraint ... will soon find in circumstances a bond of Union and will ultimately gain the confidence of the Property and good sense of the Country' (**81**).

By the beginning of 1834 Peel's political message seemed to be making some headway. The Ultras in the House of Commons, accepting his indispensability as leader, were slowly being reabsorbed into the Conservative Party; and the revolt of the moderate Whigs was already commencing. In May 1834 four members of the government, including two cabinet ministers, Lord Stanley (later the 14th Earl of Derby) and Sir James Graham, resigned over the 'lay appropriation' clauses of Russell's Irish Church Bill. This was a heavy blow to Earl Grey. Stanley was 'the Rupert of debate' and Graham an excellent administrator; and they were supported by some forty MPs, the so-called 'Derby Dilly', which Stanley hoped to weld into a 'third force' in the House of Commons (**50**). These moves were encouraging to Peel. The Whig defectors consisted of just the sort of moderates whom he wished to win to his side; and Stanley and Graham, rightly handled, would be prize catches for any future Conservative administration.

The culmination of Peel's early work and hopes in opposition came unexpectedly in November 1834 with the resignation of Lord Melbourne, Grey's successor, while Peel was away on the Continent. Wellington advised the King to send for Peel, and he himself acted as a stop-gap premier until Sir Robert was able to take over and form his first ministry in December after a hurried return from Italy. That Peel was appointed Prime Minister at all was a tribute to the unique position he now occupied within the Conservative Party; and, whatever their past differences, the new Conservative government was supported enthusiastically by the party as a whole. Though it was not outstanding in personnel — the major burden was borne by Peel himself who combined the offices of Prime Minister and Chancellor of the Exchequer — the ministry did contain four Ultras as well as new younger men like Gladstone and Sidney Herbert, and therefore marked a further stage in the consolidation of party unity. Unhappily for the Prime Minister, both Stanley and Graham refused cabinet posts. They remained suspicious of the 'liberal' credentials of the new government; it was after all Wellingtonian in its inception and the Duke remained an important member of it as Foreign Secretary. They were also reluctant as yet to break decisively with their former political associates. It was the refusal of Stanley and Graham to join the new ministry that made Peel more dependent than he wished to be on Ultra support.

Given the composition of the new administration and its status as a minority government, everything depended on its policies if it was to survive. That, as Greville commented, was unlikely to happen 'if Peel makes a High Tory government and holds High Tory language' (**12**, iii). It is this latter point that helps to explain Peel's publication of the Tamworth Manifesto on 18 December 1834, as the first salvo in the election campaign that shortly and inevitably followed at the beginning of the new year. The Tamworth Manifesto, addressed to Peel's constituents, was thus essentially an electioneering document which aimed to appeal to the electorate at large — over the heads of the ministry, as it were — by displaying the 'progressive' credentials of the Conservative Party, particularly in relation to contemporary issues [**doc. 11**]. Its authority, however, came from Peel's position as Prime Minister; and it is this, as well as its form and content, that gave it its special significance as the fundamental statement of the doctrines of Peelite Conservatism.

Though it is impossible to gauge the practical effects of the Manifesto, the Conservatives did well at the 1835 general election. They gained more than a hundred seats, and did much to recover their former position in the English counties. This meant that they had doubled their number of MPs, and, if the Whigs and Radicals are treated separately, the Conservatives now formed the largest single party in the House of Commons. This did much to give new vigour and purpose to the Prime Minister and the government; and Peel now pushed ahead with his plans for reform. His creation of the Ecclesiastical Commission gave the Anglican establishment a chance to begin the long-overdue overhaul of the finances and administration of the Church of England. Peel was also prepared to deal with some of the grievances of the Dissenters. At the same time he bluntly refused to repeal the Malt Tax, thus showing his determination not to be bullied by the leaders of special interests among the Tory rank-and-file. But in all this, as Peel realised, he was playing against time. If the Opposition could reunite their forces then the government's fate was sealed. That is exactly what did happen as a result of the notorious Lichfield House Compact, made between the Whigs, Radicals and Irish, on 28 March 1835. Within a few weeks the government was defeated on Russell's Irish Church resolutions — the price the Whigs paid for O'Connell's support — Peel resigned, and Melbourne came back as Prime Minister.

Despite the fact that Peel's first ministry only lasted a hundred days (it began and ended as a minority government) its importance for the Conservative Party was considerable from many points of view. Its constitutional implications have already been discussed. As a factor in Conservative recovery, the Hundred Days were crucial. The general election of January 1835 had done much to wipe out the ignominy of the 1832 disaster. It is in 1835 that the modern Conservative Party was really born. With 290 MPs in the House of Commons, a more effective organisation and established leaders, the Conservatives were now a formidable parliamentary force. All this helped to raise their morale and placed the Conservative Party as a whole more firmly behind the leadership of Peel, even though it is evident that only a minority of members actually embraced his progressive principles. Even the Ultras acquiesced, and now virtually disappeared as a separate group. Lord Londonderry, a leading Ultra, spoke for many of them when he wrote: 'I feel that there is but one man and one party for us now, and that is Peel' (**128**). Peel had indeed increased his stature enormously during the Hundred Days. As Prime Minister he had shown courage, energy, firmness, and an unexpected good temper in handling both his own party members and the Opposition. In the business of government he had again displayed detailed knowledge, formidable powers of work and concentration, and administrative mastery. All this won the admiration of his own party and the whole House of Commons. As Greville wrote: 'I believe it to be impossible that anything can prevent Peel's speedy return to office; he has raised his reputation to such a height during this session . . . He is indispensable to the country' (**12**, iii).

The tendencies which were at work in the mid-1830s to strengthen the Conservative Party continued unabated in the years that followed Peel's first ministry, so that their decisive electoral victory in 1841 was 'the culmination of a slow-maturing Conservative sentiment' among the English voters (**128**). The Conservative Party was now a much more coherent and disciplined body than it had been only a few years before. It is true that the Lords continued sporadically to harry Whig legislation, often in defiance of the party leadership; and it took the combined efforts of Peel and Wellington to contain their opposition within reasonable bounds. As the former complained in 1837: 'Few people can judge of the difficulty there has frequently been of maintaining harmony between the various branches of the Conservative party – the great majority in the House of Lords and the minority in the House of Commons consisting of very different elements that had been in open conflict within a recent period' (**10**, ii). In the House of Commons itself, however, there were only three occasions between 1835 and 1841 when the backbenchers revolted against Peel, and they were all on relatively minor Irish issues, a subject which, as always, acted as an irritant to Tory prejudices.

All this was in large measure a tribute to Peel's authority within the parliamentary party, but it was an authority which was shared and sustained by the work of his nominees as Chief Whips during this period (Sir George Clerk and Sir Thomas Fremantle) and their colleagues on the Conservative Electoral Committee working through the Carlton Club. Peel also relied heavily on the advice of his close associate, F. R. Bonham, the Conservative Party agent (**111**). Sir Robert also tried to ensure a better rapport with his rank and file by holding meetings of leading party members of both Houses at Westminster and at his own family house at Drayton Manor; and occasionally he summoned gatherings of the whole parliamentary party. Firm and skilful leadership and party organisation at Westminster thus clearly contributed to the healthier state of the Conservative Party after 1835, but party solidarity was also strengthened by the backbenchers' simple recognition that, with ultimate electoral victory now clearly within their grasp, it would be the height of folly to rock the party boat. As Greville observed in 1836, the Conservatives had 'visions of office . . . always ready to dance before their eyes' (**12**, iii).

Another important factor was party policy. Despite the fact that Peel made some of his greatest speeches appealing to 'enlightened' middle-class opinion during the years between the general elections of 1835 and 1837, it is the negative rather than the positive aspects of Conservatism that are most distinctive during these years. The Conservative Party was once more the resolute defender of the constitution against Radicalism. It saw the Radicals united, growing in power and importance, particularly after the Lichfield House Compact, and threatening to bend the irresolute government of Lord Melbourne to their will. This view of Radicalism was something of a myth — the parliamentary Radicals were a declining rather than an expanding force in the later 1830s — but the myth was potent enough to act as a spur to Conservative unity and morale (**24**).

There were two aspects of Whig policy that Conservatives were particularly concerned with, Ireland and Dissent: these topics divided the government and the Opposition more sharply than any others in the years down to 1841. As far as Ireland was concerned, Peel and his party were alarmed at what they considered the growing influence of O'Connell, whose anti-Union politics they detested, on the government's Irish policies; and were particularly outraged at Lord John Russell's plans for further reform of the Church of Ireland covering lay appropriation and tithe relief. The situation was similar with Dissent. What worried Conservatives was the increasingly militant mood of the Dissenters which challenged not merely the special privileges of the Established Church but, for some of them, the very notion of 'Establishment' itself. This new outlook was not only the result of the Dissenters' justified impatience at the lack of progress in remedying their major grievances, but, more fundamentally, an expression of their new dynamism in terms of growing membership, organisation, sectarian enthusiasm and social and political influence. It was the Dissenters whom the Duke of Wellington blamed, hysterically, for the 'new democratic influence . . . introduced into elections', following the Great Reform Bill (**31**). In terms of practical effect the Municipal Corporations Act of 1835 was actually much more important. The build-up of the Dissenters' social and political importance at local level, through the newly-elected town councils, is one of the significant features of provincial life in mid-Victorian England.

Not that the Whigs did very much for their religious friends during the 1830s. The three Dissenters' grievances that were most hotly debated in Parliament at this time were their lack of full control over the registration of their own births, marriages and deaths; the compulsory payment of church rate; and their exclusion from the universities of Oxford and Cambridge. A Civil Registration Act in 1836 (approved by Peel) gave them largely what they wanted over the first point; and the undenominational University of London received its royal charter; but that was all. Russell abandoned his attempt to deal with the other Dissenters' grievances, partly because Peel vehemently defended the Anglican monopoly at Oxford and Cambridge; and the Whig backbenchers were almost as stalwart defenders of compulsory church rate as their Tory counterparts. Nevertheless, the potential threat to the Anglican Church contained in the demands of Irish Roman Catholics and English Dissenters, with the apparent acquiescence of Whig ministers, proved a powerful stimulant to Conservative harmony and party zeal.

These fears also affected the moderates in the House of Commons. Sir James Graham began to work more closely with Peel after the 1835 election; though Stanley — still pursuing his mirage of a 'third force' — moved more slowly, and did not adopt Graham's position until after the next election. By the beginning of 1838, however, both men had become Peel's closest political advisers, and the 'Derby Dilly' had disintegrated, its members now finding their natural resting place within the ranks of the Conservative Party. It has been estimated that fifty-eight members crossed the floor of the House of Commons during the years of Whig ascendancy (**128**).

Peel's awareness of the importance of winning over the moderates in the House of Commons to some extent explains his tactical restraint during the mid-1830s. The fact that he was ultimately successful in gaining their support had a profound effect on party politics, for it meant that the independents were now virtually eliminated from the Lower House, and thus as many observers noted – like Gladstone, writing in 1841 – 'the principle of party . . . now has a sway almost unlimited' (**4**, ii). Indeed, for present-day historians, the strength of the two-party system is the outstanding feature of the politics of the decade 1835–45 (**45, 25, 37, 28**). The pressure of the party system itself, therefore, acted to produce conformity within the ranks of the Whigs and the Conservatives. Nor were these feelings confined to the House of Commons. 'The whole nation', wrote a contemporary observer in 1836, 'was split into two great opposing parties' (**37**); and this was reflected in the press and, particularly, in party organisation.

As we saw earlier, an *ad hoc* committee – the so-called 'Charles Street Gang' – had been set up in 1831, independent of Peel, to supervise Conservative electoral arrangements. In the following year the Carlton Club was established as the party headquarters; and it was F. R. Bonham who emerged thereafter as the Conservatives' chief electoral expert. He made his mark during the 1835 general election; and shortly afterwards he suggested to Peel the formation of a permanent committee to deal with electoral matters. 'For myself', he added, 'I am ready *to devote my whole time* out of the H of C to this work' (**111**). The plan was approved, and Bonham, whose parliamentary career soon languished, became in effect the Conservative Party's permanent political agent.

He worked from the Carlton Club in association with such leading members of the Electoral Committee as Sir Thomas Fremantle, the Chief Whip, and Lord Granville Somerset, who helped to provide the necessary aristocratic aura. These arrangements were closely tied to the political leadership, and Bonham worked closely with Peel, who gave him his full confidence and support, advising him on many matters affecting the parliamentary party. His main work, however, lay in the electoral field. Here Bonham was concerned with the registration of voters – so vital under the new electoral regime – the selection of Conservative candidates, canvassing, the press, patronage, party finance, control of the secret electoral fund – the young Disraeli, for example, received a subvention of £500 at the 1835 election – and similar matters. 'Thanks to you', wrote Sir James Graham to Bonham in 1841, 'and your indefatigable industry, no

Party out of office ever before possessed such sources of intelligence and such means for active war' (**111**).

The work of Bonham and the Carlton Committee complemented but did not supersede the activities of Conservative supporters at local level. The years after 1835 were followed by a dramatic growth of Conservative constituency associations, mainly as a result of local initiative and enterprise, itself the expression of party vigour and the strength of local political opinion. These were mainly in towns and cities, rather than in the shires where deference was stronger and more formal electoral organisation less needed. By 1841, therefore, the Conservative Party possessed 'a wide if loose array of local organisations' (**113**). Their work was much the same at local level as the more general supervision exercised by the Carlton Club nationally. They were concerned primarily with electoral registration and the choice of candidates, and were often jealous of their local autonomy and suspicious of interference from London. But grass-roots Conservatism, like Whiggism, only really sprang into life at election times; and this should warn us against attaching too much importance to party organisation in the early Victorian period. Clearly, it was both a cause and a consequence of Conservative recovery; but party organisation was 'mostly a gloss on the structure of politics' (**128**). It was more profound factors that were reshaping political allegiance in the age of Melbourne and Peel.

The Conservatives were lucky enough to be given another chance to test their growing political strength when, following the accession of the young Queen Victoria, a general election was held in 1837. That election, as a leading Tory peer observed, showed them 'increased and more than ever united' (**37**). The Conservatives fielded considerably more candidates than they had done in 1835. Their slogan of 'the Church in danger' proved a powerful rallying-cry for their troops; and partisan support for the Church of England blended in smoothly with crude anti-Irish feeling and detestation of O'Connell in the country at large. As Francis Baring, a devoted Whig supporter, admitted: 'Everything which I should call liberal . . . in Ireland has always been done against the feeling of the mass of the people in England proper . . . and O'Connell and the "Church in danger" have been the cause of our being beaten in England' (**128**). Nevertheless, it was a hard-fought election. If the Conservatives could rely in 1837 on the force of Anglican sentiment, the Whigs could expect the equally firm support of the Dissenters. Hence the Whigs were able to prevent their defences being completely overwhelmed, and Conservative gains were limited to about thirteen seats. This did mean, however, that the government's majority was reduced to just over twenty, and this placed its legislation at the mercy of Peel and the Conservative Party.

The years after 1837 formed, therefore, an unhappy period for Melbourne's government, torn between its longing for a quiet life and the importunities of its Radical supporters. As Russell neatly put it: 'If they attempt little, their friends grow slack, and if they attempt much their enemies grow strong' (**31**). Melbourne's enemies were indeed strong enough to defeat him in the House of Commons over the Jamaica Bill in May 1839, and he resigned, only to find himself quickly back in office again when Peel failed to form a Ministry owing to the young Queen Victoria's refusal to dismiss her Whig 'Ladies of the Bedchamber'.

The last two years of its life were particularly difficult ones for the Whig ministry. The country was now going through a severe period of economic and social crisis, marked by the revival of the Chartist movement and bitter hardship for the working classes, whose problems were worsened by the financial timidity and incompetence of the government which led to soaring food taxes and declining revenue. By 1841 the budget deficit had reached £6 million. Moreover, the Anti-Corn Law League, founded at Manchester in 1838, now placed the issue of the Corn Laws squarely before Parliament and the country, and therefore faced the Whig ministry with yet more uncomfortable decisions. In desperation the Cabinet eventually responded to pressure from within and without by making the Corn Laws an open question among its supporters; and in 1841 it finally came out in favour of a fixed corn duty. This was bound to push the agricultural interest ever more firmly onto the Conservative side; a tendency which had been apparent since 1835 as a result of the worries of farmers and the activities of the agricultural societies (**16**). Difficult problems in foreign and imperial affairs also harassed ministers at this time. The end came on 4 June 1841, when the Opposition won a 'no confidence' motion by one vote. Melbourne resigned; Parliament was dissolved; and the two parties squared up for the third general election within six years.

The election of 1841 was a confused affair as far as issues were concerned. 'The great struggle of the General Election', wrote one county newspaper, 'will arise from the question, of whether the Agriculturalists of the Empire shall or shall not retain that protection which is necessary to their existence' (**128**). Clearly, there was much truth in this general claim as far as the counties were concerned, and it was here that the Conservatives made their greatest mark. But the election did not turn on the question of maintaining or rejecting the Corn Laws — both parties still supported them in principle; and, as in 1837, religious fears and grievances, linked particularly with Ireland, were also important (**51**). 'Our great force', as Anthony Ashley said of his party, 'has been Protestantism' (**128**). Opposition to the Whig Poor Law of 1834 was also of importance in some parts of the North of England. Furthermore, the government's decision to reduce the timber and sugar duties in order to increase revenue by encouraging consumption antagonised important commercial and shipping interests. This lack of any great overriding issue made it tempting for contemporaries to emphasise personal factors, particularly the pre-eminence of Peel. 'The elections are wonderful', wrote Croker to the Conservative leader on 20 July, 'and the curiosity is, that all turns on the name of Peel' (**10**, ii). Formally, this was an exaggeration. Yet, insofar as Peel's name seemed to symbolise those elements of firm leadership and governmental capacity that the Whigs so conspicuously lacked and many electors admired, Croker was not far wrong. In a real sense the Conservatives had succeeded in the 1830s in winning 'the mind of the country'. As Francis Baring wrote of his own party at the time of their defeat in 1841: 'The country is against them . . . The country is tired of the old hands and wants to try a new doctor' (**128**).

The outcome of the election of 1841 was a decisive win for the Conservative Party and a personal triumph for Peel [**doc. 12**]. It was a unique result, since for the first time in British history a minority Opposition party had defeated the party of government backed by the Crown. The Conservatives obtained a majority of about eighty seats, and the configuration of the election results indicates the nature of their support. They remained the party of England: there (together with Wales) the Conservatives obtained 302 seats to the Opposition's 196. Conservative strength lay in the counties and small boroughs. In 1841 Peel's party made a net gain of twenty-nine county seats, and thus controlled 136 out of 159 county seats in England and Wales. They also obtained a majority in the smaller boroughs. The Conservatives did win forty-four seats in the larger urban areas; but these were in the older commercial centres, such as Bristol and Liverpool, rather than in the great industrial cities. It does seem, therefore, that Peel's exhortations to the new urban middle classes, as distinct from the older professional and commercial elite, fell largely on deaf ears. It was the traditional Tory slogans — the Church in danger, the Corn Laws under threat — rather than the new spirit of the Tamworth Manifesto which prevailed in 1841. This is a sombre reflection on Peel's efforts to educate his party in the 1830s (**122**). The Conservative Party still remained above all the party of the land; a fact that was to have dramatic consequences for Peel and his party in the 1840s.

3 Peel in Power, 1841−45

Peel as Prime Minister

Peel's first task as Prime Minister was to form a Cabinet, and since he was determined to reward experience and encourage party unity, its general character was not unexpected. Lord Lyndhurst, who had served as Lord Chancellor in the ministry of 1835, resumed that office, and his former colleague, Lord Wharncliffe, was appointed Lord President. The Duke of Wellington, now too old and deaf to serve again as Foreign Secretary and no longer close to the Prime Minister, was given the largely honorary post of Minister without Portfolio. Henry Goulburn (formerly Home Secretary) became Chancellor of the Exchequer, an office which confirmed his qualities as an admirable civil servant rather than a creative statesman, and where he was content to act as the executor of Peel's innovative financial schemes. Lord Aberdeen was promoted to the Foreign Office. Mild, conscientious and conciliatory, his non-Palmerstonian qualities were to prove useful assets in the future in his diplomatic dealings with France and the United States (**75**). Inevitably though, given the overwhelming domination of domestic problems and policies during the 1840s, foreign affairs had little impact either on the progress of Peel's ministry or the Conservative Party itself.

Particularly gratifying to Peel personally was the entry of the two ex-Whig Ministers, Stanley and Graham, into the Cabinet. Viscount Stanley became Colonial Secretary; but the office itself had now declined in importance, and the temperamental aristocrat soon proved to be an uneasy colleague in the Lower House. In 1844 he was 'kicked upstairs' to the more congenial atmosphere of the House of Lords. Sir James Graham obtained the more rewarding post of Home Secretary. This turned out to be a major appointment (**94**). Graham's political outlook and interests were close to Peel's. The problems of the age meant that not only was the work of the Home Department at the very centre of the ministry's activities, but that Sir James and the Prime Minister had the opportunity to work closely and amicably together. Graham's unsympathetic manner in the House of Commons made him a less than popular figure there; but he was an outstanding administrator — painstaking, intelligent and, in his own terms, effective. It is true that he was temperamentally pessimistic, and faced with outbreaks of working-class violence in the first year of the ministry's life, and worried about Ireland, he tended to see 'plots' and 'conspiracies' everywhere. But in practice he exercised his responsibility for law and order with firmness and efficiency. Sir James Graham became in effect 'Number Two' in the government.

To conciliate the agriculturalists Peel brought into his Cabinet their two outstanding parliamentary spokesmen, the Duke of Buckingham (Lord Privy Seal), and Sir Edward Knatchbull (Paymaster-General). As Cabinet Ministers neither had much to commend them. The irascible Buckingham soon resigned over Peel's first budget; and Sir Edward followed him in February 1845, by which time (as Greville grumbled) he had shown himself to be 'entirely useless . . . and earned universal contempt in the House of Commons' (**12**, iv).

Peel also promoted a number of outstanding younger men who had served in the 1835 ministry; notably Sidney Herbert, who became Secretary to the Admiralty, and W. E. Gladstone (now rapidly abandoning his youthful High Toryism) as Vice-President of the Board of Trade. Gladstone was lucky as well as talented. The fact that his chief, the Earl of Ripon, was in the Lords, and a lethargic administrator, meant that much of the detailed work of planning and executing Peel's free trade programme fell into the capable hands of the Vice-President, an onerous task he performed with skill and enthusiasm. As a result Gladstone was promoted to the Presidency of the Board of Trade with a seat in the Cabinet in 1843.

As a whole, therefore, Peel's government was an exceptionally strong one in terms of personality, experience and administrative ability. Three of its members – Stanley (later the fourteenth Earl of Derby), Gladstone and Aberdeen — were future Prime Ministers. Politically, however, its outlook was blunter. Even before the final crisis of 1846, ministers failed to gauge accurately the temper of the House of Commons on a number of key issues; and on the wider political front they were largely insensitive to the real significance of movements such as Chartism and the Anti-Corn Law campaign. In its strengths and its weaknesses, however, as in its personnel, the government was essentially 'Peel's Ministry'; he had created it and in the end he was to destroy it. It was Peel who gave it unity, coherence and direction, through his personality, his authority and his policies. But, as with the later Conservative governments of Neville Chamberlain and Margaret Thatcher, that very domination — the fact that the Prime Minister had no real intellectual challenge from his colleagues — produced its own problems for the Conservative Party.

In the summer of 1841 Peel was at the height of his powers. Like Churchill in August 1940, he could argue that 'all my past life had been but a preparation for this hour and for this trial'. Now aged fifty-two, masterful and confident, he possessed a wealth of knowledge and experience of government and administration stretching back to the early years of the century. Like all great Prime Ministers he had an abundance of physical energy and enormous powers of work. This meant that though he was sustained by the active support and devotion of a number of key figures in the government, especially Graham, Aberdeen and Gladstone, it was Peel who set the pace and controlled the work of the administration. He possessed moreover a remarkable mastery of government business and the work of the major departments. He generally introduced his own budgets, for example, and was almost as deeply involved with the major preoccupations of the Home Office as Sir James Graham himself. As Gladstone said of him, he was 'the best man of business who was ever Prime Minister' [**doc. 13**].

As Prime Minister, Peel was responsible not only for formulating policy, but for explaining and defending it in the House of Commons; and there, as earlier, with his lucidity, control, and mastery of his material, he often excelled. Peel was indeed a superb parliamentarian; as Disraeli said he could 'play upon the House of Commons like an old fiddle'. His emphasis on the House of Commons as *the* great political forum of the nation did make him unsympathetic to the activities of the great pressure groups of the period. Again, like every Victorian Premier, Peel was forced to dispense patronage, particularly in church affairs, a task he detested. As he protested to Croker after a few months in office; 'his life is one of toil, and care and drudgery', whose only comfort is its 'means of rendering service to his country, and the hope of honourable fame' (**7**, ii).

Peel was not only Prime Minister, he was also head of the Conservative Party. Everything conspired to make Peel an authoritarian leader: his temperament, his consciousness of his own abilities, the enormous demands on his time and energy as head of the government; above all his long-held views on the role of the 'Queen's Ministers' and their relationship to the House of

Commons. For he believed that the responsibility of a Prime Minister, even one who had gained power through an impressive electoral victory, lay primarily to the Queen, the nation, and his own conscience; only secondarily to the Conservative Party. He refused, he said, referring to the claims of his party, to be subject to such an 'odious servitude' (**10**, iii). The duty of a Conservative government was to govern; the purpose of the Conservative Party in the House of Commons was above all to support that government in carrying out its arduous tasks with its votes. If it failed to do so, then it would have to accept the consequences. A responsible Prime Minister, Peel insisted:

> 'will not condescend to humiliating submission for mere party purposes; will have neither time nor inclination to be considering how many men will support this public measure, or fly off to gratify some spite or resentment; he will do his best for the great principles that his party supported and for the public welfare, and, if obstructed, he will retire from office, but not from power; for the country will do justice to his motives, and will give him the strength which his party had denied to him' (**7**, ii).

Such a 'high' view of the Prime Minister's office was particularly difficult for a Conservative leader to sustain in the 1840s. For the Conservative Party had emerged in opposition after 1832 as a 'Church and State' party, committed to opposing any further changes in the political system or the established rights of the Church of England. It was partly its successful resistance to such changes that brought it to power in 1841. But, as Gash has stressed: 'It was the fate of the great Conservative party of 1841 . . . that the problems it had to face when it came to power were not the problems it had been created to solve' (**45**). The 'good old causes' of the 1830s which had helped to unite the party retreated into the background; the new issues of the 1840s were those linked with the 'Condition of England' question — finance, trade, employment, poverty and social reform. For Peel these were essentially national, not party, problems, especially since his attitude to them was primarily intellectual and related firmly to the orthodox economic philosophy of the time. Such questions should therefore be handled with the cool rational expertise of the experienced administrator, rather than being subjected to the ignorance and rhetoric of the backbenchers. It was these new issues, Peel believed, that provided both a test and an opportunity for the aristocratic governing class of England to prove its value and its vigour.

But their very range and complexity, the emotions they aroused, the special interests and prejudices they touched upon, made the problem of maintaining party discipline and unity in relation to such economic and social questions an extraordinarily difficult one, especially as the Peelite Conservatives were only a minority within the parliamentary party. Backbenchers were not only alarmed at the implications of some government measures in the 1840s; they resented the apparent aloofness of ministers — their refusal to explain or justify government policy — and the coldness and arrogance of Peel. Often they felt that they were regarded only as voting fodder to troop obediently through the lobbies in support of government bills. 'Peel has committed great and grievous mistakes', wrote Lord Ashley in 1843, 'in omitting to call his friends frequently together to state his desires and rouse their zeal . . . men would have felt they were companions in arms; they now have the sentiment of being followers in a drill' (**128**).

These were problems, however, which lay in the future. Whatever the later views of his Conservative critics, Peel assumed office in the autumn of 1841 with enthusiastic party support, and the strong feeling in the nation at large that he was the one man who could tackle forcefully the major problems that faced the country. Peel was confident that he could justify that trust.

Social distress and disorder

The situation that now faced him was a grim one. Not only were the nation's finances in a parlous state; since 1838 the country had been suffering from the depredations of profound economic depression after the relatively prosperous years of the earlier 1830s. Wheat prices rose from an average of 35*s* 4*d* a quarter in 1835 to 73*s* in 1838, and remained over 60*s* a quarter until 1842. High food prices for the labourer were accompanied by declining prices and profits particularly in the cotton industry, ever the index of British economic progress. The industrial working classes, especially in Lancashire, were faced therefore with wage cuts, short-time working, heavy unemployment, and desperate living conditions; relieved only by recourse to private charity and a local poor relief system which was clearly collapsing under the strain. Social distress was particularly acute in 1842 shortly after Peel took over: 'no gloomier year existed in the whole of the nineteenth century' (**32**). Graham reported to the House of Commons that more than a million people were in receipt of poor relief in England and Wales out of a total population of 16 million. Peel himself commented on the dreadful poor relief figures for the cotton town of Paisley in Scotland. What added to the anxieties of the Prime Minister and his second-in-command was the fear that the desperation and bitterness of the industrial workers would be exploited by the leaders of the great radical movements of the time and erupt into violence and disorder. No wonder that Peel and Graham in 1842 have been called 'haunted men' (**130**)!

Already in the later 1830s opposition to the new Poor Law had become a focus for working-class discontent in the North, aided and abetted by radical Tories such as J. R. Stephens and Richard Oastler, who were associated also with the movement for factory reform (**17**). But the anti-Poor Law agitation — which was successful in slowing down the introduction of the new system in the northern counties — was now overtaken by movements which in the eyes of the government were much more dangerous; notably, the Anti-Corn Law League and a revived Chartism, both prepared, at the very least, to use powerful and provocative language to get their message across to the public.

Yet the government's fears of provocation were perhaps exaggerated. It is true that the revival of the Chartist movement in 1841–42 was in many ways impressive: a new National Charter Association was established; local Chartist committees were active especially in the North, Midlands and Scotland, spurred on by the oratory of O'Connor (after his release from prison in the summer of 1841) and that of other Chartist leaders also. The result of all this was the planning of a new National Chartist Convention to meet in London in April 1842, to be followed by the presentation of another great National Petition to the House of Commons in favour of the famous 'Six Points'. That petition was presented in May, and inevitably rejected by a massive majority. Peel dismissed the Chartist demands as mere 'trash and delusion': any advance towards manhood suffrage would, he argued, mean the destruction of the 'balanced constitution', and, besides, would the granting of the vote to the working man do anything to improve his standard of life? (**11**, iv). For Peel, quite simply, Chartism was not a political but a public order problem. Indeed, the rejection of the petition meant that the Chartist movement was halted in its tracks; and the leadership was forced once again to reconsider its tactics (**71**).

In some ways the position of the Anti-Corn Law League was similar. The League had been remarkably successful since its foundation in 1838 in converting middle-class opinion to its case against the Corn Laws. Its more recent policy of electoral intervention also seemed to be paying dividends when a handful of freetraders were victorious in a number of industrial constituencies in the North and the Midlands in the general election of 1841. Richard Cobden won at Stockport; a victory which now made him the effective leader of the anti-Corn Law forces in the House of Commons. But after the decisive triumph of Peel and the protectionist party in that election, the one great aim of the League — the total abolition of the Corn Laws — seemed further away than ever; especially as the implications of Peel's own financial and commercial reforms in 1842, including the new Corn Law, appeared to weaken the credibility of the League's all-or-nothing policy. If the League was undermined on the right by Peel, it was also hammered on the left by the rivalry and unremitting hostility of the Chartist leaders, especially O'Connor. Like them, the League Council too was faced with a problem of tactics after 1841—42. 'I am told on all sides that, unless we do something . . . we shall lose public confidence,' lamented Cobden. '*What can we do?*' (**20**).

When working-class violence did break out in the summer of 1842, it was due more to long-pent-up resentment against intolerable economic conditions than to the direct effects of outside political pressure. It was sparked off by a strike of Staffordshire miners over a wage dispute in early August, and this was followed by similar actions over the next few days in most of the industrial areas of Great Britain. The centre of the troubles, however, lay in the English textile regions. There, at Stalybridge in the heart of the industrial north-west, where a number of masters were planning wage cuts, the workers came out on strike on 5 August and brought the life of the town to a standstill. The strikers then planned to encourage 'turn-outs' at all the local factories in the area through marches and demonstrations and thus bring about a general strike. Their ultimate aims were confused, but centred on the traditional claim for 'a fair day's work for a fair day's wage', and many also showed strong support for the People's Charter. The pressure for a general strike was largely successful, and this was soon extended into the city of Manchester itself. By mid-August some 50,000 workers were out; the turn-outs then spread into South Lancashire and Cheshire and across into many of the woollen towns of Yorkshire (**61**).

Inevitably, the progress of the turn-outs and strikers, though reasonably well-organised, was accompanied by intimidation and sporadic violence with some destruction of property and loss of life. At some factories the men drew the plugs from the boilers to make sure that work stopped; hence the name 'the Plug Plots' which was given to the movement (**130**).

The initial reaction of Sir James Graham to these events was one of horror. He spoke of the 'mad insurrection' of the working classes, and was convinced that the movement was directed and spurred on by a dedicated band of conspirators, influenced by Chartism and associated with the Manchester Trades Conference [**doc. 14**]. All this was reminiscent of 1817. But the Home Secretary was no Lord Sidmouth. In practice he behaved calmly, firmly and sensibly, and his actions were strongly backed by Peel. As the Prime Minister insisted, in his typically blunt way: 'to preserve peace, to put down plunder and to prevent the forced cessation of labour by intimidation are the sole objects of the Government' (**94**). Graham believed, therefore, in relying in the first instance on the local magistracy, police and constables. But the feebleness of many Lancashire magistrates in dealing with the disorders led to the despatch of troops to the areas where it was clear that law and order was breaking down. There clashes between the soldiers and the populace did lead to some loss of life. At the same time Graham tried to stiffen the efforts of the local guardians of the law and men of property to do more for themselves. 'Gentlemen and mill-owners . . . must take some trouble . . . they must incur some risk. If they will not do this, they must bear the consequences . . . Government will do what they can, but they cannot be everywhere and do everything' (**90**, ii). His policies soon proved effective. By 23 August the worst rioting was over. Sullenly the men began to return to work, and the industrial districts were more or less back to normal by the end of September. Helped by a good harvest in 1842 and the beginnings of improvement in trade, the turn-out movement was over by 1843.

Yet it had important long-term consequences both for the government and the radical opposition. Graham was determined in the aftermath of the Plug Plots to make the 'conspiracy' charge stick against both the League and the Chartists. 'We are on the track of the real authors of the mischief', he told Peel on 24 August 1842. At Graham's suggestion the government's case against the Anti-Corn Law League was set out by J. W. Croker in an article in the *Quarterly Review*. As Croker indicated, the League leaders *had* employed inflammatory language in denouncing the aristocracy and prophesying revolution before the turn-outs occurred. It is also true that an extremist group had proposed shutting factories or refusing to pay taxes as a means of forcing Peel to abolish the Corn Laws. Some League members too, led by Joseph Sturge, had attempted to establish an alliance with the Chartists on the basis of common support for free trade and suffrage reform, though this move soon collapsed. Again, as Graham pointed out during the troubles, some magistrates who were supporters of the League readily acquiesced in, even if they did not actually encourage, the turn-outs in their towns. But in the end the leaders of the Anti-Corn Law League drew back from the precipice and turned against the strikers; partly out of self-interest — many were factory masters themselves — but also because of the strong influence of Cobden in favour of moderation and independence. The League had learnt its lesson. By the end of 1842 it was back on course and stronger and more confident than before (**20**).

The position of the Chartists was far otherwise. The National Charter Association meeting in Manchester in the summer of 1842 was caught unawares by the actual outbreak of unrest in Lancashire, but once the turn-out movement got under way, O'Connor and most of the Chartist leaders were prepared to jump on the bandwagon and give direct support and encouragement to the strikers. This gave the government the opportunity it had been waiting for to break the back of the Chartist movement by the arrest, trial and imprisonment of its leaders. In this it was only partially successful. Legal problems and delays meant that though O'Connor and other Chartists were eventually convicted and imprisoned, they were released soon afterwards. Nevertheless, the Chartist involvement in the Plug Plots certainly contributed to the decline of the second phase of the movement until its final re-emergence and collapse in 1848 (**62**).

Despite the action taken by the government against those held responsible for violence and disorder in 1842, both Graham and Peel were anxious not to appear to be acting as apologists for the employers, for whom Sir James particularly had no great regard or respect. As he wrote to Peel, 'they must not play the game of the League by reducing wages and increasing profits at the expense of the working man, the master being protected by military force' (**10**, ii). Peel himself supported an inquiry into the grievances of the Staffordshire miners. The Plug Plots thus did something to arouse the social conscience of the government; though Graham, characteristically, had little faith in pure legislation to remedy the deep-rooted evils of an industrial society.

More importantly, the revelations of working-class distress and discontent in the summer of 1842 confirmed for Peel the wisdom of the economic strategy upon which he had already embarked. It was the underlying causes of social distress, he argued, that must be tackled; and this could only be done by radical financial and commercial reform. 'Something effectual must be done', he wrote, 'to revive the languishing commerce and manufacturing industry of this country . . . We must make this country a cheap country for living . . .' (**10**, ii). These were the economic aims that Peel set himself in the course of the next four years.

Finance and free trade

After the years of financial drift and ineptitude displayed by the Whigs, Peel saw tax reform as his main priority when he assumed office in September 1841. Drastic measures were needed, he believed, to overcome the financial deficit – 'this mighty and growing evil' – bequeathed to him by Lord Melbourne, a sum which *in toto* now approached £7 millions. Peel was now convinced that the re-introduction of the income tax was the only and inevitable solution to this problem; he had in any case always believed in the merits of direct taxation (**118**). Unpopular it might be, but its overwhelming advantage was that it guaranteed a certain yield of revenue; and, during a period of profound social distress, a tax on income possessed the additional merit of falling wholly on the wealthy rather than upon the poor. Though both Stanley and Graham were opposed and Goulburn was unenthusiastic, after lengthy discussions and consultations outside, the Cabinet was eventually won over to the Prime Minister's proposal. After briefly meeting the Commons to secure essential credits, Parliament was adjourned for three months while Peel worked out the details of his budget proposals. Nothing was yet known about his intentions. 'The aristocracy and the people', Cobden wrote, 'are gaping at him, wondering what he is going to do' (**20**).

He began, early in 1842, by first tackling the thorny question of the Corn Laws. Here he aimed at fair rather than excessive protection, bearing in mind the various interests involved – agriculturalist, manufacturer, consumer. The 1828 Corn Law had failed to provide that stability of prices which was one of its main aims, and its level of duties seemed unnecessarily high. Peel's new Corn Law therefore reduced the duties on the sliding scale for corn and refined its operation. Though Peel insisted after the passage of the Act that its provisions were 'in conformity with my own convictions', it was in many ways a political rather than an economic gesture, especially as his original proposals were slightly modified in a protectionist direction by the Cabinet. He hoped for the moment to damp down controversy by yielding a little to the moderate opponents of the Corn Laws without antagonising overmuch the agricultural protectionists, and riding out the predictable storm of abuse from the Anti-Corn Law League. Thus he would gain time and support to push through his wider, more innovative, economic programme. In all this he was largely successful: but only at the price of evading rather than confronting the fundamental issues raised by the protracted Corn Laws controversy.

Peel introduced his plan for an income tax as part of a masterly Budget speech presented to the House of Commons in March 1842 [**doc. 15**]. He proposed a tax of 7*d* in the pound on incomes over £150 per annum, as a temporary measure, and he anticipated that it would produce an annual revenue of between £3 and £4 million; in fact it raised nearer £5 million. In recommending the measure the Prime Minister appealed to the sense of justice (and self-preservation) of the propertied classes. The working classes, he intimated, would recognise the innate fairness of such a direct tax compared with the heavy burden of indirect taxation that they bore; especially as Peel made it quite clear that the introduction of the income tax was to be coupled with a drastic programme of tariff reduction, particularly on articles of general consumption. All this, he believed, would stimulate manufacture and commerce, encourage employment and reduce the cost of living for the poor. Financial and commercial reform would thus help to encourage national unity and harmony and undermine political discontent; an aim which was underlined (as we have seen) by the outbreaks in the northern industrial districts a few months later. Peel's purpose in his great Budget of 1842 was thus as much social as economic.

As far as his general tariff policy was concerned, Peel was committed to a programme of moderate free trade through the reduction of duties. The groundwork had already been prepared by the earlier reforms of Huskisson and Robinson, which Peel had strongly supported; and by the anti-protectionist sentiments of 'enlightened' opinion, as represented by, for example, *The Economist*, and the officials of the Board of Trade (**14**). Influential too was the report of Joseph Hume's Select Committee on Import Duties (1840), which showed how obstructive and irrelevant in terms of revenue yield the majority of them were. Over 90 per cent of customs revenue was obtained from a handful of articles. In his Budget speech Peel therefore suggested the reduction of import duties on raw materials to 5 per cent; on semi-manufactured articles to 12 per cent; and on foreign manufactured goods to 20 per cent; the duties on a miscellaneous group of some 750 imports (including cattle and meat) were to be lowered, as were those on foreign and colonial coffee and timber. Export duties on domestic manufactures were also to be reduced.

Like the income tax, Peel's commercial proposals were generally welcomed in the Commons, where they were passed eventually by a majority of more than a hundred. It was difficult for his opponents to refute convincingly much of the detailed evidence and argument he presented. The only real opposition came from a group of Tory agriculturalists. If they had earlier shown 'coldness and indifference' (according to Greville) to the new Corn Law, they were now more belligerent in their condemnation of the proposed reductions in the duties on imported farm produce. 'They do not care for the income-tax nor are they very rebellious about wheat', wrote one Lincolnshire MP to the Prime Minister, 'but on barley and oats and cattle they are, with reason, dissatisfied' (**81**). One hundred and thirteen Conservative backbenchers showed their resentment by voting for William Miles' resolution opposing the cattle duties. Peel was irritated but undeterred. 'To their demand', he wrote, 'I could not, I cannot accede. I have a deep impression, a firm conviction, that population is increasing more rapidly than the supply of provisions in this country, and that no advantage can be derived by the agriculturalists from keeping up higher duties than I propose' (**104**).

In fact Peel believed, as he wrote to Croker later in the year, that 'the Tariff does not go far enough' (**10**, ii). One of his problems was that the fruits of the new financial and commercial revolution were slow in coming; there was still a budget deficit, for example, in 1842−43. In the following financial year, however, the tide was clearly turning. Trade and industry were recovering, and Goulburn was able to report a surplus of just over £4 million, some of which was used to reduce interest charges on the National Debt. Duties were also abolished on raw wool, and reduced on coffee and sugar, though the last proposal only got through the Commons after a dramatic confrontation between the government and a refractory section of Tory backbenchers. With these reforms may also be associated the Bank Charter Act of 1844, which, by extending the powers of the Bank of England over note issue, aimed at ensuring a more stable financial system.

The way was therefore prepared for Peel's final Budget in 1845, 'a masterpiece of administrative planning' (**81**). Income tax was renewed for a further three years, though the government had now achieved a revenue surplus of £5 million, and this gave the Prime Minister the opportunity to deliver an even more uninhibited onslaught on the principle of protection than in 1842. Nearly all remaining import duties on raw materials were abolished, and duties on a whole range of foodstuffs were abolished or reduced. Export duties on manufactured goods disappeared.

Overall, Peel's financial and commercial programme was proving an undoubted success, even though free trade was a stimulus to rather than the primary cause of the economic recovery that was clearly visible after 1843. Politically, however, within his party, the consequences were less satisfactory. The implications of Peel's economic strategy exacerbated rather than tempered the mood of 'sulky disaffection' which, as a result of other government decisions, was beginning to dominate the outlook of many members of the parliamentary Conservative Party.

Social reform

For a variety of reasons the problems of social reform were bound to be an important preoccupation of Peel's ministry. The principle of state intervention to remedy some of the worst abuses of the industrial system had already been accepted by the Whig governments and the legislature in the 1830s. The great Factory Act of 1833 limited the hours of work of children and young persons in textile factories − since it was accepted that they were not free agents, no economic law was violated − and in addition authorised the appointment of factory inspectors. The following year the much-hated new Poor Law Act was passed; and in 1839 the Whigs increased the state grant for education. The advent of bitter industrial depression after 1838, and the radical protest movements associated with it (anti-Poor Law agitation, short-time committees demanding the ten-hour day, Chartism, the Anti-Corn Law League) all helped to keep alive the social question. This, together with the fact that important government-sponsored reports on working conditions were already in the pipeline when Peel took office, meant that the new Conservative government was certain to be faced very quickly with important decisions in the field of social reform. And if ministers were hesitant in their reactions, then there were a number of Tory MPs, notably Lord Ashley − passionate and indefatigable in his support for factory reform − who were prepared to act as spurs to the government's conscience.

Yet both Peel and Graham, the minister primarily responsible, were likely to be cautious social reformers. Graham's rigid commitment to the principles of laissez-faire and his Malthusian pessimism about the possibility of social improvement, together with his obsessive concern with problems of law and order and administrative detail, made him unsympathetic to the grievances of the working classes (**106**). Though Peel was personally more concerned, in practice his attitude did not differ that much from his Home Secretary, and as always it was he who set the tone of the Conservative administration. Peel also accepted almost without question the current economic philosophy: 'all direct interference of the government', he had said earlier when he was Home Secretary himself, was so much 'quackery' (**118**). Above all, since he believed profoundly that the best hope for the well-being of the working classes lay in expanding British commerce and manufacture, social reform was merely for him a subsidiary palliative; it must be justified rationally in relation to the wider needs of the economy. Peel's whole economic outlook made him more amenable, therefore, to the arguments of the anti-interventionist manufacturers rather than those of the factory reformers; and indeed, to the exasperation of Ashley, he refused in 1842 to commit himself in principle to support for the ten-hour day. It was not unexpected, therefore, that in the same year Sir James Graham renewed the Poor Law Act for a further five years. It was observed sardonically by one Radical MP that those Tories who had waxed so indignant about the evils of the Act during the election campaign of the previous year, were now 'mute as mice' (**124**).

The first real test for the administration's social conscience came in 1842 when the report of the Royal Commission on Children in the Mines appeared. The revelations of the ghastly conditions in the industry (driven home by the graphic illustrations) shocked public opinion and made legislation inevitable. The government did not oppose Ashley's Mines Bill, which proposed the banning of children under thirteen and of women working underground, and it passed the Commons easily; but they gave it no positive encouragement. Indeed, two members of the Cabinet, Wellington and Wharncliffe, opposed the Bill in the Lords; and, at the instigation of the great coalowner, Lord Londonderry, a series of amendments were passed there, notably the notorious clause reducing the age of exclusion from thirteen to ten. These amendments were quietly accepted by Peel, and it was the modified Bill that became law the same year.

In 1843 Graham turned to the factory question, but with extraordinary political naivité he introduced a Bill which 'combined the nitro of factory reform with the glycerine of the educational issue in one explosive package' (**106**). Ashley was prepared for the moment to forgo the ten-hour day and accept the Home Secretary's reform for the sake of children's education. But the question of factory hours was swept away by the furore created by the latter proposals. As Peel correctly forecast to the Queen: 'The High Church party is not satisfied with the bill; but their opposition will be less formidable than that of the Dissenters' (**81**). Graham's Bill proposed compulsory part-time education for the factory children· and though, as far as responsibility for the teaching was concerned, he aimed at concessions from all the interested religious parties, it was clear that in practice the Anglican Church would gain most from the scheme. The Dissenters responded by a powerful nationwide campaign against the Bill. Graham bowed to the storm, abandoned the Bill and with it, for the moment, the prospect of factory reform. The end result of the *débâcle* was not only to weaken the reputation of the government — 1843 was a bad year all round for Peel — but to increase the general distrust and unpopularity of Graham even within the ranks of his own party. 'He was', said Ashley, 'the most dishonest of all public officers' (**79**).

Some resolution of the factory-hours question was imperative. It was kept alive by the reports of the government's own inspectors as well as the agitation of the short-time committees; and in the House of Commons, Ashley — for whom the ten-hour day was essential to the 'welfare of the working classes and the real interests of the country' (**79**) — was determined to push that claim. In February 1844 Graham introduced a revised Factory Bill which abandoned the notion of compulsory education and confined itself to proposing a further reduction in children's hours to six-and-a-half, but a twelve-hour day for young persons and women, now to be brought within the scope of legislation. The insistence on twelve hours outraged Ashley. At the Committee stage in March he introduced his famous ten-hour amendment in a passionate speech in which he detailed the humanitarian case for the proposed reform. Implicit in his argument, as everyone realised, was the almost certain assumption that a ten-hour day for women and young persons would necessitate a ten-hour day for men. Hence Graham in his reply attacked the amendment, entirely on economic grounds: he dilated on the injurious effects of such a radical reduction in hours on capital, Britain's competitiveness and upon the operatives' wages [**doc. 16**].

Peel himself later addressed the House, in a speech which Ashley not unfairly called 'ingenious in argument but wretched in principle and feeling', since it failed to confront head-on the positive arguments for the ten-hour day in textile factories, and adopted a hectoring tone which was resented by many (**85**, ii). Hence on 15 March Ashley's amendment was passed by 179 votes to 170, a majority of nine against the government.

How had the ministry got itself into such a plight? For Peel it is clear that the factory-hours question was much more than a simple humanitarian issue. He believed, wrongly, that the ten-hour day would have damaging effects on British industry generally and inhibit the economic recovery on which his sights were set; but he was moved as much if not more by political considerations. For a largely landowning Parliament to set itself up against the wishes of the manufacturing interest was both unwise and dangerous; for it was likely to fuel the resentments of the Anti-Corn Law League, by 1844 an increasingly influential body both inside and outside the House of Commons. And behind all these arguments there was, in the end, Peel's long-held presumption that it was the duty of the parliamentary Conservative Party to support the Cabinet once it had made up its mind on a major issue. As he put it starkly to the Queen, shortly after the original government defeat: 'Your Majesty's servants are in a minority, but they consider it would be inconsistent with their public duty to sanction or acquiese in the views of the majority' (**10**, iii). Ashley's tactical triumph did not therefore change the government's stance. Peel, Stanley and Graham opposed any compromise, despite the fact that some members of the Cabinet – Gladstone especially – argued in favour of an eleven-hour day and were supported in this by a representative group of manufacturers. The Home Secretary insisted publicly on his 'insuperable objection' to a ten-hour Bill.

After much parliamentary confusion and recrimination, Graham introduced a new Bill in May which reiterated the twelve-hour principle. Ashley replied with a ten-hour clause. 'The House is summoned', he proclaimed, 'to cancel its vote, not upon conviction, but to save a Government' (**85**, ii). It was a shrewd thrust. Both Graham and Peel now threatened the Commons with resignation unless the government's twelve-hour clause was supported. This pressure did not change more than a handful of the original anti-ministerial votes, but it did bring to heel the abstainers and absentees of 15 March. On the decisive vote on 13 May the government obtained a comfortable majority of 138. The Factory

Bill then became law in June 1844 with the twelve-hour clause for women and young persons intact, and a 'half-time' day for children.

The ministry got little credit for what was, after all, a considerable reform. The whole long-drawn-out affair revealed once again Graham's ineptitude in handling the House of Commons, and the drawbacks of the politics of confrontation especially when faced with a man of the character and integrity of Ashley. It also showed, all too glaringly, Peel's authoritarian view of the relationship between the executive and the legislature. This constitutional conviction, together with the aloofness of the Prime Minister and his senior colleagues in their dealings with their backbenchers, made it almost certain that sooner or later they would be faced with another party revolt.

Ireland

Together with the 'Condition-of-England' question, Peel also inherited from his Whig predecessors the Irish problem. 'We have', he observed early in his new ministry, 'that great standing evil which counterbalances all good, the State of Ireland' (**81**). By 1842 little had been done to remedy the fundamental social and religious problems of that country, which Disraeli was to summarise in memorable words in a Commons debate in the following year as 'a starving population, an absentee aristocracy and an alien Church' (**74**). Politically, however, Ireland had been fairly quiet in the 1830s. This was mainly the result of O'Connell's deliberate policy in the aftermath of his triumphant campaign in 1829 in favour of Roman Catholic emancipation. He now commanded a small Irish party of some thirty MPs in the House of Commons, and though his long-term aim was clearly repeal of the Act of Union, in typically opportunist fashion the 'Liberator' was now prepared to concentrate on an immediate programme of Irish reform, partly to conciliate his moderate middle-class supporters. Fears of further unrest in Ireland, together with an acceptance of the legitimacy of many Irish grievances, made the Whig ministers amenable to the case for reform.

In 1832 Stanley, as Irish Secretary, introduced a system of 'national schools' which, though it failed to satisfy his aim of overcoming religious sectarianism, did much to attack basic illiteracy. The following year the Irish Church Act slimmed down the unrepresentative Church of Ireland by abolishing ten sees, including two archbishoprics; but Russell's controversial proposal

that the sequestered funds should be used for secular purposes —
the notorious 'lay appropriation' clause — was dropped, owing to
ministerial disagreements and the opposition of the Lords, supported by Peel. The Lichfield House Compact of 1835 strengthened
O'Connell's hand, and was followed by further Irish reforms. In
particular, Russell, as Home Secretary, attempted to introduce the
new English system of local government into Ireland, and in
principle this was accepted by Peel. But once again the Upper House
refused to tolerate the vital provision of ratepayer suffrage, and the
final Irish Corporations Act of 1840 was a much narrower measure
than its English counterpart. In the end, therefore, the Irish Roman
Catholics gained little of real substance from a decade of Whig reform; and this was largely due to the fact that ministers, though
well-meaning, were unprepared to tackle the fundamental problem
of the opposition of the House of Lords where the Conservatives
had a built-in majority. As Peel admitted, in relation to Whig legislative proposals, this gave him 'power with irresponsibility' (**53**).

It was impossible to expect, therefore, that O'Connell would stick
to his strategy of reform once the Conservatives came into office in
1841. Nor was there any sympathy or understanding between the
Irish leader and Peel upon which a parliamentary accord could be
built; there was rather an antipathy which went back to the days of
the latter's Irish Secretaryship nearly thirty years earlier. Even
before the Whigs left office O'Connell had veered back to support
for repeal. In 1840 the National Repeal Association was established
in Ireland, backed by the peasantry, many of the middle classes,
and, significantly, by the bulk of the parish clergy — a key factor in
the development of the movement (**121**). Indeed, despite
O'Connell's links with English radicals and the support of a handful
of Protestant nationalists like Thomas Davis and William Smith
O'Brien, leaders of 'Young Ireland', both the 'Liberator' and repeal
became closely identified with the aims and aspirations of the
Irish Roman Catholic Church, much to the disgust of diehard
Protestants. Fundamentally, the Association was a vast pressure
group which aimed (like the contemporary Anti-Corn Law League)
to arouse and canalise opinion through propaganda and large-scale
public agitation, and thus force the government to repeal the Act
of Union. 'O'Connell chose to use extra-parliamentary means to
achieve constitutional ends' (**68**); a tactic which had after all worked
successfully against another Tory government in 1829.

Yet Peel was in a much stronger position in 1841 than Wellington
had been during the Emancipation crisis. The Irish electorate was

no longer so formidable, owing to the earlier disfranchisement of the forty-shilling freeholders. Nor was O'Connell's support as united as it appeared: 'Young Ireland' (as later events showed) differed sharply from the 'Liberator' over tactics and long-term aims, and moderate Catholics were worried by the radical implications of a mass repeal movement (**57**). By contrast, all shades of Protestant opinion in England and Ireland were totally united in their opposition to repeal. To begin with, therefore, Peel was prepared to countenance a policy of 'benign neglect' (**104**); to tolerate the repeal movement so long as it remained strictly within the law. He therefore played down the alarmist clamour of Lord de Grey, the strongly anti-Roman Catholic Lord Lieutenant, and the Irish Protestants for immediate suppression of the Association. Yet certain cautionary measures were taken. In a set speech to the House of Commons in May 1843 (repeated in the Lords) Peel spelt out the implications of his support for the Union. 'Deprecating as I do all war, but, above all, civil war, yet there is no alternative which I do not think preferable to the dismemberment of this empire' (**30**). At the same time the army was strengthened in Ireland. Clearly, on this occasion the government was determined not to back down.

On the other hand, Peel constantly applied pressure on de Grey and other members of the Irish administration to adopt a more liberal attitude in the appointment of moderate Roman Catholics to official posts; supporting a limited policy of what today would be called 'positive discrimination' in their favour. 'What is the advantage to the Roman Catholics', he wrote to the Lord Lieutenant in September 1843, 'of having removed their legal disabilities, if somehow or other they are constantly met by a preferable claim on the part of Protestants, and if they do not practically reap the advantage of their nominal equality as to civil privilege?' (**10**, iii).

As far as the repeal campaign was concerned, things came to a head in the autumn of 1843. The momentum of the movement itself pushed O'Connell and the other leaders into more threatening postures, with hints of mass unrest and military action. Peel waited for the right tactical moment to arrive, and then pounced. The great meeting planned by O'Connell to take place at Clontarf on 7 October was banned by the authorities. The Irish leader accepted the decision peacefully, and his followers acquiesced. It was a turning point in his work for Ireland. Already ageing, the 'Liberator's' career now went into permanent decline, worsened by his arrest and imprisonment in 1844, even though the verdict against him was soon quashed by the House of Lords (**59**). Yet all was not lost. The work of the Repeal Association at least, O'Connell suggested, 'aroused the English nation from slumber', and led to a new period of Irish reform initiated this time by the Irish leader's *bête noire* Sir Robert Peel.

The lesson that Peel drew from the confrontation of 1843 was that 'mere force, however necessary the application of it, will do nothing as a permanent remedy for the social ills of Ireland' (**10**, iii). What he aimed at now was to build up in Catholic Ireland a feeling of confidence in the effectiveness and impartiality of government and the law, and thus reconcile the community to the benefits of the Union and the maintenance of the Anglican Establishment. This could be assisted, he believed, by the Irish administration applying a more deliberate policy of appointing suitable Roman Catholics to official posts, particularly in the judiciary. At home too, the Prime Minister submitted to the Cabinet in 1844 a programme of wide-ranging Irish reform, covering such controversial topics as the franchise, landlord/tenant relations, and Catholic education. The immediate purpose of the whole reform package was, as he said in his cabinet memorandum: 'to detach (if it be possible) from the ranks of Repeal, agitation and disaffection, a considerable portion of the respectable and influential classes of the Roman Catholic population' (**10**, iii). The Irish middle classes would thus help to leaven the mass. What Peel also had in mind was the need to break the 'powerful combination' (as he termed it) of O'Connell and the Catholic clergy — the dynamic behind repeal. It was this, suggests a recent historian, that provided 'the cornerstone of his Irish policy' (**121**). It helps to explain the extraordinary, and unsuccessful, attempt by the British government to obtain the Pope's unequivocal condemnation of the political activities of the Irish priesthood.

The Prime Minister's programme of Irish reform began symbolically in 1844 with the replacement of the diehard Protestant Lord Lieutenant, de Grey, by Lord Heytesbury, a colourless but more liberal figure, and a new Irish Secretary was also appointed. The new administration did do something to encourage the wider appointment of Roman Catholics to judicial posts, though this cut little ice with the community. The first important legislative change proposed by Peel was his Charitable Bequests Bill. Its intention was to establish a new Board of Bequests (to replace an older Protestant-dominated one) which would contain Roman Catholic members, and aim at encouraging private bequests to help the sorely-stretched finances of the Roman Catholic clergy. At first the scheme was strongly opposed by the hierarchy, but in the end the support of a number of leading Catholic bishops enabled the plan to go forward. It was a small but significant victory for Peel. It represents his 'initial attempt to enter into a working relationship with the Catholic bishops [which] would open the way for the rest of the programme of conciliation and weaken the massive clerical support for O'Connell' (**121**).

Other parts of Peel's programme were less successful. A proposed new Franchise Bill, based on a five-pound-freeholder franchise, gained little support in the House of Commons and was dropped. The government now accepted that there were desperate conditions among the Irish tenantry and serious problems in their relations with the landlords. In 1843 it had set up a Royal Commission under the Earl of Devon to investigate the whole subject. The Devon Report of 1845 was and remains an exhaustive treatment of the state of Irish landholding on the eve of the Great Famine, but for the moment its evidence led nowhere. Peel introduced a Bill that proposed compensation to evicted Irish tenants for improvements made to their holdings; but it quickly succumbed when faced with the Lords' adamantine principle of 'no interference with the rights of property'. As Graham commented: 'Alas! I fear that the remedies are beyond the reach of legislative power' (**10**, iii). These failures meant that Peel's reform programme came to centre more and more on the improvement of Irish education, and in particular on the vexed question of state support for the training of Roman Catholic priests at Maynooth College.

Maynooth College had been established by the Irish Parliament in 1795 as a training college for Roman Catholic priests, an alternative to the potentially subversive atmosphere of the seminaries of revolutionary France. After the Union the college was supported financially by an annual parliamentary grant of £9,250 — with no strings attached — and this remained the position down to the 1840s, even though its inadequacy was becoming clearly apparent. Indeed, in 1842 the Conservative government still insisted on leaving things as they were. In the course of the following year, however, Peel changed his mind, and began to discuss with his closest colleagues the possibility of increasing the Maynooth grant. This was not only part of his general policy of conciliation in Ireland; he also hoped that a greater injection of state funds into the college would encourage the rise of a more 'respectable', less politicised class of parish clergy. The penury and backwardness of the college, he argued, 'all combine to send forth a priesthood embittered rather than conciliated by the aid granted by the State for their education, and connected . . . with the lower classes of society' (**10**, iii). In 1844 he brought the question before the Cabinet and was supported by a majority of its members, though Goulburn and Gladstone were opposed. The latter eventually resigned in the following year, for obscure intellectual reasons of his own.

In suggesting increased state help for Maynooth the government was embarking on a difficult course. As Graham pointed out to Peel: 'I foresee that on the part of the British public in their present temper, invincible repugnance will be felt to any such proposal' (**10**, iii). By the 1840s, mainly as a result of increased antipathy to the Irish and fears engendered by the Oxford Movement, the country was probably more anti-Catholic than it had been a generation earlier. Hence when Peel's Maynooth Bill was presented to the House of Commons in April 1845, it was greeted by a storm of protest throughout the United Kingdom. The provisions themselves were moderate: Maynooth College was to receive a permanent annual grant of £26,000, together with an immediate capital sum of £30,000. Nevertheless, despite the fact that the state had been subsidising Maynooth financially for half a century, the proposed Bill brought out into the open two principles – state support for religion, and the encouragement of the Roman Catholic Church – each of which offended powerful religious and political groups.

Hence the government found itself faced by an extraordinary rag-bag coalition of forces against the Bill: Tories, Low-Church Anglicans, Orangemen, Dissenters and Radicals. The influential Protestant Association, particularly outraged by the Prime Minister's refusal to provide grants for Anglican religious purposes, formed the Central Anti-Maynooth Committee, which represented both Anglican and Dissenting clergymen, and mounted a formidable propaganda campaign against the government's proposals (**66**). As a result petitions against the Bill (in Macaulay's phrase) 'showered thick as a snow-storm on the Table of the House'. *The Times* thundered: 'It is not Liberalism but Romanism which Peel is forcing on the nation . . . It is not merely Popery, that is unpopular enough in England, especially Irish Popery, but it is Maynooth. It is a name and a thing above all others odious and suspicious to England' (**121**).

Within the House of Commons Peel found himself opposed by an important section of his own party, many of whose members had consistently voted against the annual Maynooth grant in the past. The opposition of the Conservative Party in the Lords, led by Irish Ultra peers such as Roden and Londonderry, was even more virulent and scurrilous (**53**). Nevertheless, Peel was determined to proceed. 'This Bill must pass. I will concentrate all my efforts to pass it' (**10**, iii); a sentiment which was shared in Ireland by the Lord Lieutenant. Rejection would mean, wrote Lord Heytesbury to the Prime Minister, 'every bad passion will be roused — the Roman Catholics will unite again as one body, the force and power of the Agitators will be enormously increased' (**121**). In the end the Maynooth Bill passed in the spring of 1845, but only as a result of the firm support of the Irish, and of the Whigs in both Houses of Parliament. The Conservative vote in the Commons was very closely divided: on the second reading, 159 for and 147 against; on the third reading, 149 for and 148 against.

From a party point of view Peel seemed to have behaved over Maynooth even more stubbornly and impetuously than he had done during the two earlier crises in 1844 over the Factory and Sugar Duties Bills. 'All this raises a storm', he wrote to Croker on 22 April, during the final phase of the Maynooth Bill, 'at which I look with much indifference, being resolved on carrying the Bill, and being very careless as to the consequences which may follow its passing, so far as they concern me' (**7**, ii). As far as Ireland was concerned the results of the Maynooth Act were not very dramatic, though it did do something to enhance Peel's policy of conciliation and slightly improve his popularity there. In English politics, on the other hand, the consequences were profound. Maynooth proved to be an important turning-point in the relations between Peel and his party, an aspect which is discussed in more detail below. With the Maynooth problem out of the way, Peel could now move on to the final phase of his Irish programme — the Colleges Bill. This passed fairly easily through Parliament (though O'Connell opposed it) and led to the establishment of university colleges at Belfast, Cork and Galway, thus providing wider and cheaper opportunities for higher education in Ireland. But the aim of interdenominational teaching was once again, as over the 'national schools', bedevilled by religious sectarianism.

How important then was Peel's work for Ireland? It is possible that it did something to reconcile the two communities; but even that small advance was swept away by the horrors and bitterness of the Great Famine in 1846. Peel's reforms certainly displayed the Prime Minister's courage and resolution: as the most recent historian of the subject writes, 'considered in the context of the time and the prejudices of his own party they were remarkable' (**121**). But as a long-term solution to the problems of Ireland, Peel's reform programme was hopelessly inadequate. Nothing was done to alter the status of the Church of Ireland. Nothing was done for economic improvement or land reform. Like factory reform, Ireland shows the limits of Peelite Conservatism.

4 Conservative Opposition to Peel, 1841–45

Conservative opposition to Peel during this period arose out of two main areas of policy. On the one hand there were the old traditional issues of dispute, agriculture and religion, rooted deep in the past; on the other, there were the new social questions which only really emerged in the 1830s, the Poor Law and, more especially, factory reform. Each cause had its devoted supporters. There was a hard core of about sixty MPs who formed a more or less permanent opposition to Peel over his agricultural policies; another group of some fifty MPs opposed him over religion; and roughly the same number over social issues. There were of course no hard and fast divisions between these groups: Lord Ashley, for example, was prominent for his concern over both factory reform and the future of Protestantism. Nor, as Peel often hinted, were his opponents' criticisms completely disinterested; personal animosities, self-interest and political ambition all played an important part. What all this meant was that most Conservative opposition between 1841 and 1845 manifested itself, as it usually does, at a practical rather than a theoretical level: by opposition in Parliament to particular ministerial proposals, rather than through the development of a coherent anti-Peelite political doctrine. Nor did votes against the government necessarily mean that the Conservative backbenchers involved wanted either to bring the ministry down or to display their lack of confidence in Peel.

One group who were in many ways opposed to Peelite Conservatism were the 'Tory Radicals', as they have been called, men such as Sadler, Oastler, Stephens, Busby Ferrand, and the Reverend G. S. Bull – 'Parson Bull of Bierly' (**22**, **78**). All of them were associated with industrial Yorkshire; all (with the exception of the Wesleyan, J. R. Stephens) were fervent Anglicans; and as a group they were more important 'out of doors' than within the House of Commons. Their devotion to 'The Altar, the Throne and the Cottage' (in Oastler's slogan), their emphasis on the values of hierarchy, authority and paternalism, meant that Richard Oastler and his friends regarded themselves as old-fashioned Tories, firmly opposed to 'the Demon called Liberalism' and its progeny, political reform and Roman Catholic Emancipation (**78**). On the other hand they hated the rapidly-advancing industrial system, on both political and humanitarian grounds. It uprooted traditional social relations and values and spread subversion and discontent. At the same time it replaced the old personal relationship between masters and men by the impersonal cash-nexus, the by-product of utilitarianism and *laissez-faire*. 'God's laws', said Oastler, 'must bend and break at the call of avarice and self-interest' (**23**). In their social outlook, therefore, the Tory Radicals were, literally, reactionaries. It was the evils of the new industrial order they were combating, and they gave their support to its victims – paupers, factory children, industrial labourers.

The Tory Radicals were heavily involved in the movement for factory reform. Oastler's famous letter of 1830 on 'Yorkshire Slavery' had helped to precipitate a new phase of activity, and Michael Sadler was the protagonist of the ten-hour Bill in the House of Commons in 1831–32. In the later 1830s, however, after the enactment of the compromise Whig Factory Act of 1833, their efforts were largely directed to attacking the new Poor Law. For the Tory Radicals the 1834 Act appeared to be the epitome of all they detested in the new England. It marked the expansion of centralised administration at the expense of the old parochial system of poor relief. 'I am so far a Conservative', said Stephens, 'that I do not wish to see the old English institutions destroyed' (**116**). Even more, it attacked 'the birthright of the poor' – the natural right of the labourer to work or relief.

Yet, as with the rejection of the ten-hour day, the Poor Law Act of 1834 was passed by an overwhelming majority in parliament. No Conservative leader, and only a handful of their backbenchers, voted against it, despite the fact that it offended many deep-rooted party instincts; the prospect of a dramatic fall in the poor-rate burden was too alluring (**19**). Nor did Oastler and his friends receive any official party backing for the great anti-Poor Law crusade they helped to mount in the north of England in 1836–37 – 'the apogee of Tory Radicalism' (**17**). It was not to be expected then that the Tory Radicals would welcome with any great expectations the new Conservative government of 1841. 'I fear there is something rotten, out of joint and ricketty about it', exclaimed Oastler (**23**). He mistrusted Peel's commercial outlook, and saw little difference between new Conservatism and old Whiggery. He and his friends were pessimistic about the prospects for future factory reform and despondent over Graham's renewal of the Poor Law Act in 1842, which Busby Ferrand attacked in a blistering speech. Nevertheless, as before, the government's action was supported by an enormous majority.

Indeed, in terms of influencing government policy or the views of the Conservative Party as a whole, the Tory Radicals were in a difficult position. Their archaic social outlook meant that they had few practical remedies to offer for the pressing problems of the 1840s; while the outspokenness of their language and their earlier association with working-class radicals and Chartists alarmed some otherwise sympathetic Conservatives. Most important of all perhaps was the simple fact that their only representative in the House of Commons after 1841 was Busby Ferrand (Sadler had died in 1835 and Oastler was in prison for debt) and he was neither admired nor trusted. What this meant, therefore, was that the leadership of the social reformers on the Conservative side of the House passed into the hands of Lord Ashley, a man whose membership of the aristocratic landowning class made him a very different figure from any of the Tory Radicals, even though his social and religious outlook had much in common with theirs.

Ashley's humanitarian impulse sprang not from any hostility to industrialism *per se*, but rather from his Evangelicalism which, he believed, necessitated the application of Christian principles to the practical problems of society. Morality, rather than political expediency, must be the rule. This was an attitude of mind which was poles apart from that of his fellow-Conservatives and Anglicans, Peel and Graham; and this fact, together with his long and steadfast commitment to the ten-hour day, meant that his relations with the two ministers were bound to be fraught with difficulties. Indeed, both Peel and Ashley got off on the wrong foot from the very start. In forming his new administration the Prime Minister offered Ashley a minor post in the royal household. This was rejected, primarily because Ashley felt that membership of the government might inhibit his support for that 'great national question', factory reform. Ashley had in fact already tried to obtain from Peel a personal commitment to the ten-hour day, which the Prime Minister refused, though he indicated to the zealous reformer that he could go ahead on his own if he wished. Ashley was convinced that the government had no intention of supporting a ten-hour Bill; and that, therefore, as he told Bonham, he would be driven into taking 'a hostile and active course' against the ministry (**109**). This almost led him to break publicly with the Conservative Party, though in the end he drew back from that step.

Nevertheless, in 1842–44 he found himself increasingly out of tune with the government's social policy. 'Imports and exports, here is Peel's philosophy! There it begins and there it ends', he wrote in September 1842. And in the following month, in words reminiscent of the Tory Radicals: 'All Peel's affinities are towards wealth and capital . . . What has he ever done or proposed for the working classes . . . Cotton is everything, man nothing'. He dismissed the record of Peel's ministry: 'men looked for high sentiments and heard small opinions; for principles and were put off with expediency' (**79**). As Ashley's latest biographer suggests, this viewpoint was not entirely fair to Peel. Ashley was an independent backbencher, who looked at ministerial policy entirely from the point of view of his own obsessive concerns, to which he was able to devote almost all his time and energy. Peel was an overworked Prime Minister forced to deal with the whole gamut of governmental and party affairs. Even so, as far as the welfare of the working classes was concerned, it was means rather than ends that divided the two men. Ashley pinned his faith in immediate social improvement; Peel, as we have seen, was concerned with the longer-term conditions of economic prosperity. Neither really appreciated the other's attitude (**79**).

Ashley's opposition to the government came to a head in the debates on the Factory Bill of 1844, when, in reply to the proposal for a twelve-hour day for women and young persons, he insisted on putting forward his ten-hour amendment. This was passed by 179 votes to 170. As Greville noted, the opposition vote seemed to cut across party and sectional divisions [**doc. 19**]. It was supported by Whigs, Radicals and Irish, and about ninety Conservatives, made up mainly of agriculturalists, determined — as Peel suggested to the Queen — to show their hostility to the manufacturers of the Anti-Corn Law League (**10**, iii). But even a few Peelites were with Ashley, including Viscount Sandon and the Yorkshire MP, J. S. Wortley. It is true that only a minority of the party voted against the government. Nevertheless, the vote does show the restiveness of a wide cross-section of Tory backbenchers in the face of ministerial stubbornness, and the strength of feeling over the factory-hours issue. Sandon wrote to Peel of 'a widely extended feeling in favour of a restriction of the hours . . . that had reached quarters that it had not reached before' (**22**); and Gladstone, no friend of factory reform, made a similar observation in Cabinet.

As we have already seen, Peel and Graham were nevertheless determined not to give way, and after the Easter recess introduced a new Bill which, under threats of resignation, was passed by a large majority. Ashley commented: 'Utterly, singularly, prodigiously defeated by a majority of 138!! The House seemed aghast, perplexed, astonished. No one could say how, why and almost when'. In fact he went on to answer his own query by adding: 'Such is the power and such the exercise of Ministerial influence . . . the majority was one to save the Government . . . not against the question of Ten Hours' (**23**). The great Evangelical might protest — 'Alas is Peel everything? Is God nothing?' – but his own analysis was undoubtedly correct. Moral considerations gave way before the brute facts of political power. For the moment at least, as Greville observed, Peel was 'the only statesman in whom the great Conservative body had any confidence or could have any hope' (**12**, v).

Another group who in some sense opposed Peel on grounds of principle was the quartet of Tory MPs known as 'Young England' (**107**). Young England originated with two aristocratic Englishmen, contemporaries at Eton and Cambridge, the Hon. George Smythe (later Lord Strongford), and Lord John Manners, eldest son of the Duke of Rutland. In speeches and writings they developed a romantic Toryism based on a bizarre version of English history, which stressed the traditional links between aristocracy and people in opposition to the harsh materialism of the commercial and manufacturing middle classes, and their allies the Whig oligarchs (**95**). All this embodied an attitude towards society which made them unsympathetic to Peel, the hard-headed son of a master cotton-spinner. Both Smythe and Manners were by 1841 members of the House of Commons, and there they were joined by another Cambridge friend, Alexander Baillie-Cockrane, and soon afterwards the new member for Shrewsbury, Benjamin Disraeli. By 1843 the Young England quartet was established as a sort of 'Fourth Party' in the House of Commons, acting together, often as gadflies to the party leadership.

The accession of Disraeli was regarded as something of a catch. Older, cleverer, and apparently more politically influential than the others, both Smythe and Manners were prepared to accept him as the leader of what was intended to be a small exclusive group. 'Dizzy has much more parliamentary power than I had any notion of', wrote Smythe naively to Lord John in October 1842 (**74**). For his part, Disraeli was prepared to go along with his younger associates since their colourful Toryism strongly appealed to him; he elaborated it in his own inimitable way in his first social novel, *Coningsby*, in 1844, where the eponymous hero is modelled on Smythe. But he also believed that they could help him to build up his political career at a time when great new issues and opportunities for debate were being opened up in the House of Commons. 'I already find myself without effort the leader of a party, chiefly of the youth and new members', Disraeli told his wife (**74**). The importance of the Young England movement lies, therefore, not in the personalities of the Cambridge trio, none of whom made their mark in politics; nor in their ideas, soon blown away by the grim realities of the age, but in 'the emergence of Disraeli as a parliamentarian of the first rank' (**128**).

'I have had to struggle against a storm of political hate and malice which few men ever experienced', wrote Disraeli to Peel in September 1841, appealing for office in the new government (**88, ii**). This was an exaggeration. But it is true that in attempting to gain entry into the House of Commons in the 1830s, Disraeli had against him his reputation, his manner, and his race. It was only when he decided to throw in his lot with the Tory Party that he was eventually returned for Maidstone in 1837, after a series of dismal failures to obtain election as an independent Radical. After his maiden speech was howled down — in one of the most famous scenes in modern parliamentary history — Disraeli learnt to temper the extravagance of his style, and was able over the next few years to carve out a reputation as a skilful and witty Commons speaker and make himself known to the party leaders.

He was deluding himself, however, after the Conservative triumph in 1841 in imagining that he would be considered for office by Peel. He lacked both experience and influence. Nevertheless, Disraeli was bitterly disappointed by Peel's rejection: he was after all now thirty-seven, an advanced age in those days for a new aspirant for office. It was this rebuff that helped to push him towards Young England in 1842—43 and made him more critical of Peel, at a time when the Prime Minister was harassed by a whole range of problems and was personally unpopular with many members of the parliamentary Conservative Party.

It was Ireland that first drove Young England into revolt. Both Smythe and Manners opened the attack. In August 1843, in a speech criticising the government's Irish Arms Bill, Disraeli first showed his outstanding parliamentary calibre and his facility for getting under Peel's skin. As Graham commented to Croker: 'With respect to Young England, the puppets are moved by D'Israeli, who is the ablest man among them . . . D'Israeli alone is mischievous; and with him I have no desire to keep terms. It would be better for the party, if he were driven into the ranks of our open enemies' (**7, ii**).

That was not to happen, yet. For the remainder of the year Disraeli made a point of supporting the government, in response to conciliatory moves from Peel. But this *rapprochement* was unlikely to have been helped by the publication of *Coningsby* in May 1844, with its famous attack on Peelite Conservatism as government through 'Tory men and Whig measures' [**doc. 17**].

That same year Young England distinguished itself by voting with the majority against the government in support of Ashley's ten-hour amendment in March, though Smythe dissented; and again on Miles' amendment to the Sugar Bill in June. When in response to the latter vote Peel and Graham threatened to resign unless the vote was rescinded, Disraeli responded with a defiant speech; he declared that he had no intention of 'changing my vote within forty-eight hours at the menace of a Minister' (**74**). In the end the Prime Minister had his way. For the remainder of 1844 Disraeli was in the north of England collecting material for his novel *Sybil*; a tour which was also marked by a series of set speeches at the Manchester Athenaeum by himself, Smythe and Manners, on the ideas of the group, which were enthusiastically received. 'Young England', announced *Fraser's* journal in 1844, 'has renovated the whole surface of things, both in politics and literature' (**22**).

In 1845 Disraeli moved into virtually open revolt against Peel. His parliamentary speeches were now marked by an acrid hostility which seemed to spring less from the political situation itself than from some deep personal resentment. Indeed, now aged forty-one, Disraeli believed that his career was standing still, and Peel — who had rejected him for office four years earlier — became the target for his frustration. In February 1845 he reproved Sir James Graham for his conduct in authorising his Home Office officials to open the mail of a Radical MP suspected of subversion. In his defence of the Home Secretary, Peel referred to Disraeli by quoting Canning: 'save me from the candid friend'. Disraeli turned the verse against Peel with devastating effect, leaving him 'stunned and stupified'. The same deadly technique was employed with equal force in a debate on the Corn Laws in the following month. In his speech Disraeli commented ironically on the difference between the Prime Minister's attitude to the agriculturalists when in opposition and now in office, and he ended with the famous apothegm, 'a Conservative government is an organised hypocrisy' (**74**).

Over Maynooth, Young England was divided: Smythe and Manners supported the government, but Disraeli voted against. His opposition speech was one of his most brilliant and earned cheers from both sides of the House; but (as Blake suggests) his arguments against the government's proposals to increase the college grant were illiberal and unsound [**doc. 18**]. For Young England the division over Maynooth was fatal. It marked in effect the break-up of a group whose unity was always suspect; Smythe in fact was soon to join Peel's government as Under-Secretary at the Foreign Office. For Disraeli it set the seal on his growing reputation as a brilliant Commons speaker and an unrivalled critic of Peel. But his achievement in 1845 was essentially a personal one: he was still very much an outsider in the House of Commons — rootless, unrepresentative and mistrusted. It was those critics of the Prime Minister who spoke for important sections and interests within the Conservative Party who, in the end, were to be the greater threat to his leadership and policies.

The greatest of these interests was of course agriculture. As Lord Ashburton wrote to Peel on his accession to office in 1841: 'I am aware to what extent our Conservative party is a party pledged to the support of the land, and that that principle abandoned the party is dissolved' (**10**, ii). Peel really needed no reminding of the political importance of the agricultural interest. He was well aware that the farmers had now become a major electoral force, partly as a result of the notorious Chandos clause of the Great Reform Act which enfranchised £50 tenants-at-will; and they were determined to use that power in defence of the system of protection. Following in the footsteps of the earlier farmers' Protectionist Societies, which had been instrumental in the passing of the original 1815 Corn Law, they now formed Agricultural Associations and other pressure groups, often under the patronage of members of the aristocracy, notably Lord Chandos, the 'Farmers' Friend' (**16**).

This politicisation of the farmers was seen in their electoral role in the later 1830s. Their fears that the Whigs were not absolutely sound on the Corn Laws issue led them to move steadily towards the Conservatives. In the general election of 1835, for example, the Whigs, who had won 102 county seats in 1832, lost 29 and gained not one; and this trend continued even though Peel had peremptorily refused to repeal the Malt Tax during his brief 'Hundred Days' in power. It was strengthened by the formation of the Anti-Corn Law League in 1838; and by the decision of the Whigs just before their exit from office in June 1841 to support a fixed duty on corn.

Hence, as we have seen, the Corn Law question was an important feature of the 1841 electoral campaign in the counties, where the result was a triumph for the Conservative Party, and overall a parliamentary majority. They gained 136 county seats compared with the Whigs' twenty-three. The *Bucks Herald* declared that the election had 'vindicated the Farmers' rights, by returning to Parliament a more decided majority to support the Corn Laws than ever before' (**16**). Yet, early in 1842, Peel was determined to introduce a new Corn Bill based on fair rather than excessive protection; and as his proposals showed, this did involve some reduction in the duties on the 1828 sliding scale. The agriculturalist MPs, however, accepted the Bill, mainly because they felt that the unity of the party and the strength of the government ought not to be imperilled at a time of widespread economic and political discontent. Their loyalty and unselfishness received scant support from their constituents. The strength of feeling displayed by the farmers at their representatives' desertion — 'all Lincolnshire is aflame' wrote one farmer — meant that in any future dispute over government policy, the agriculturalists in the Commons would have to take note of their constituents' pressure and demands. Indeed, shortly after this the Duke of Buckingham (fomerly Lord Chandos) resigned from the ministry.

Hence the county MPs voiced their opposition to Peel's proposed reductions in the duties on imported farm produce in his May Budget. The revolt against the government came to a head on 23 May when William Miles introduced an amendment against the proposed cattle duties, which was supported by 113 Conservative backbenchers. 'He and his friends', said Miles, 'had gone along with the right hon. Baronet as far as they could; they had not opposed the Corn-bill; they had agreed to it in silence. But the time of silence was now passed: it was their duty to their constituents to defer no longer stating their sentiments on this part of the measure' (**16**). Peel stood firm; and the amendment was in fact defeated by a large majority.

One should not make too much of the incident, despite the numbers involved. As D. R. Fisher argues, the sentiments of Miles and his friends are not to be taken completely at face value. They felt the need to express, sincerely, the views of their constituents; but they had no wish to embarrass the government or to have their opposition votes regarded as a lack of confidence in Peel (**108**). A similar point may be made in relation to the furore aroused among the farmers the following year over the proposed duty reductions on Canadian corn. Once again there was a revolt against the government by a tiny group of agriculturalist MPs; but this was almost a token gesture to appease the farmers' fury. As William

Yates told Peel: 'all the Cons. *want* (but you know all this) to vote with the Govt. but they are afraid of offending their constituents' (**108**). Their attempt to serve two masters was a difficult one. Lord Sandon appealed to Peel to make allowances for the dilemma of the agriculturalists 'who wish no mischief, but would be glad of an escape' by some sort of compromise (**108**). But the Prime Minister again refused to budge, and the Canada Corn Bill passed with a large majority.

Nevertheless, the fears and pressures from the shires would not go away. It was the general liberal tendency of Peel's commercial legislation that alarmed the farmers, and produced the uneasy feeling that in some indefinable way their interests were being betrayed. 'The stream of our fortunes', wrote one Lincolnshire farmer at this time, 'is careering away in an impetuous torrent towards the open gulf of Free Trade; we must stem it, quickly and with energy, or we are lost' (**16**). This was a mood that was enhanced by the renewed strength of the Anti-Corn Law League. The outcome of the agriculturalists' frustration was the formation in 1844 of the Central Agricultural Protection Society, the so-called 'Anti-League', a national alliance of farmers and landlords to defend protection, led by the Dukes of Buckingham and Richmond (**64**). Its influence in that year was small. The local farmers' societies still remained the heart of the Protectionist movement; and 1844 was a year when other matters elbowed the Corn Laws off the parliamentary stage. Peel, moreover, went out of his way in a debate in June to affirm his 'solemn and unqualified opposition' to 'the immediate removal of the present protection on agriculture' (**11**, iv). The agriculturalists' case against the government was thus based on fears for the future rather than present danger; and Peel's brusque manner in dealing with their grievances only added to their suspicions. Their irritation came out therefore indirectly in debates on other subjects: on factory reform (where they provided the bulk of Ashley's Conservative supporters) and on the Sugar Duties Bill in June 1844.

The problem of the sugar duties was a tricky one for Peel from many points of view. The British West Indies, which had almost a monopoly of the home sugar market as a result of a preferential tariff, was unable to keep up with the accelerating demand. But alternative sources of supply were not easy to come by, owing to the government's commitment to import only 'free' (i.e, non-slave-grown) sugar. Moreover, the West Indian sugar interest was a powerful one, whose commercial privileges had been supported by successive administrations; and sugar itself was *the* major source of customs revenue. Nevertheless, Peel was determined to cut the duties on both imperial and foreign sugar, in order to reduce the cost of living for the working classes and open up new sources of supply. The present duties were 25s per cwt on British colonial sugar and 63s on foreign; in his Sugar Bill Peel proposed to reduce them to 24s and 34s respectively.

The Bill was opposed not only by the West Indian interest, but also by many MPs who saw it as an unjustified attack on the principle of imperial preference and a breach of faith by the government. The attack on the government was led by Philip Miles, the protectionist member for Bristol, whose brother had played a similar role in the revolt over the cattle duties in 1842. On 14 June he introduced an amendment to reduce the proposed colonial duty from 24s to 20s, thus cleverly retaining the principle of duty reduction but coupling it with a greater differential against foreign sugar, in order to appeal to a wide spectrum of opinion in the Commons. Miles was supported by sixty-two Conservatives, and the amendment passed by twenty votes. Peel was furious. Only three months earlier he had been defeated over Ashley's ten-hour amendment, and here was the House of Commons once again twisting the ministry's tail! This time the crisis was even more serious, since it was impossible to re-introduce the Bill that session, and it soon became clear that the majority of Conservative dissidents were unlikely to change their votes. An impasse was reached. Once again, however, Peel was prepared to throw down a challenge to his party. At a meeting of Conservative backbenchers on 17 June he threatened to resign forthwith unless the vote was rescinded. His abrasive speech was much resented, but it was followed by a more emollient one by Stanley, and in the end on 20 June Peel won the day with a government majority of twenty votes.

In some ways the Sugar Duties crisis was a storm in a teacup; 'a special case, one of detail not of principle', as Lord Sandon told the Prime Minister. The sixty-two Conservative dissidents, though they contained an agriculturalist core, were a heterogeneous group; nor were they in any conscious sense attempting to overthrow the government. What brought the Conservative backbenchers to heel on 20 June was the stark reality of Peel's threat to resign, underlined by Stanley and others, which concentrated their minds wonderfully on the appalling prospect of a Whig government if he did. The sugar crisis thus demonstrated the effectiveness of Peel's ultimate sanction 'as a practical instrument for sustaining him in power' (**108**). The anti-government vote of 14 June — and earlier — represented not a factious opposition to Peel, but resentment at some of his policies and especially at the way in which they were presented to the House of Commons. The backbenchers were also asserting the right to independence of judgement for themselves and their constituents. William Miles 'could assure the Government that he held the high Conservative principles they professed; but, at the same time, he reserved to himself the gift of exercising his judgement freely and independently' (**108**). It was a point of view which was affirmed by a resolution passed at the Carlton Club at the very height of the crisis by a meeting of the whole parliamentary Conservative Party.

To some extent Peel went along with this demand for 'independence' in a later more conciliatory speech to the party. But this did not really alter his view of what an administration had the right to expect from its supporters. 'Declarations of general confidence will not, I fear', he wrote on 17 June in reply to Lord Sandon, 'compensate for that loss of authority and efficiency which is sustained by a Government not enabled to carry into effect the practical measures of legislation which it feels to be its duty to submit to Parliament' (**10**, iii). Clearly, two different views of the nature of 'party' and the role of the House of Commons were at odds here. But it was Peel's faults of manner and speech that made the situation worse than it need have been. One Conservative backbencher (later a Peelite) wrote of the Prime Minister at this time: 'He is asking from his party all the blind confidence the country gentlemen placed in Mr. Pitt, all the affectionate devotion Mr. Canning won from his friends . . . without himself fulfilling any of the engagements on his side' (**128**). Hence, though the Sugar Duties crisis was not really about the survival of the government, it did provide for the agriculturalists one more cause of resentment against the Prime Minister. Gladstone was convinced after the events of 17 June that 'a deep wound had been inflicted on the spirit and harmony of the party: a great man had committed a great error' (**4**, iii). The Maynooth controversy in 1845 was to rub salt into that wound.

Maynooth raised important questions affecting the relationship of Church and State; and was thus of intense concern to the Conservative Party, the traditional defender of the rights of the Church of England. Peel, however, was a moderate and undogmatic churchman, and his whole approach towards religious questions was that of the experienced statesman, concerned with political realities rather than theological ideals. In particular, he came to feel that the old eighteenth-century notion of the union of Church and State was no longer viable in the aftermath of the repeal of the Test

Acts, and the Catholic Emancipation Act of 1829. The Anglican establishment must be defended, but on pragmatic rather than theoretical grounds; and its members could no longer expect that its privileges would be supported by the state as of right. 'In these times', wrote Peel, 'it is not being prudent to lay down general and unqualified doctrines with respect to the essential attitudes of the Church – unless we are quite sure they are safe doctrines and true doctrines for all parts of the Empire' (**33**). Peel's sceptical tone was due to his awareness of how important liberal opinion was becoming in the earlier nineteenth century; and liberals saw the Church of England as a privileged and reactionary institution, to be reconstructed rather than defended. Even more alarming was the expansion of Dissent in terms of both numbers and influence; and Dissenters were vehemently opposed to the continuance of any special favours by the state to the Church of England. The collapse of Graham's Factory Bill in 1843 under the weight of Dissenting opposition to its educational clauses showed how powerful a force they had become.

Peel believed, therefore, that in the changed atmosphere of the times, Anglican leaders ought to be circumspect in the demands they made on the state. It was no longer politically feasible to expect even a Conservative Prime Minister to countenance the provision of state funds for the building of churches, as Lord Liverpool had done to the tune of one million pounds in 1819; though most Anglican clergymen and many Conservative MPs, such as the outspoken member for the University of Oxford, Sir Robert Inglis, felt it was the duty of the state to do just that. 'I dread for the sake of the Church and its best interests', wrote Peel to Graham in 1842, 'stirring up that storm, which large demands on the public purse would make. Ireland, Scotland, Dissent and religious indifference might be brought by skilful management to combine against a vote for Church Extension in England' (**10**, iii). It was not that Peel was against church extension, as his successful introduction of the New Parishes Bill of 1843 shows; but he stressed the importance now of voluntary contributions by the Anglican faithful.

More positively, Peel was convinced that to survive in an increasingly hostile world, the Anglican Church must purge itself of its more blatant evils – pluralism, inequality of clerical incomes, and so on – and, given the weaknesses and divisions within the Church, this could only be done under the aegis of the state. Hence his establishment of the Ecclesiastical Commission in 1835, which represented both clergy and laity and did much to advance the cause of church reform over the next decade. For the Prime Minister it represented an admirable example of church-state cooperation, and he personally contributed much to its deliberations during his ministry of 1841–46 (**33**). Yet not all Conservatives were happy with Peel's record in church affairs, as Croker reported. For some he was still to be condemned for his 'betrayal' of 1829; while his support for church reform both here and in Ireland and his sympathy with some Dissenters' grievances, only added to their doubts.

All these fears and prejudices came to a head in 1845 with Peel's plan for increasing the state grant to the Irish Roman Catholic training college at Maynooth, for it went far beyond any programme of church reform and seemed to strike at the fundamental Conservative principle of support for the Established Church, which had been reiterated in the 1830s, not least by Peel himself. Maynooth was, claimed one Anglican clergyman, 'a formal recognition of the Roman Catholic religion as a religion fostered and protected by the State' (**67**). But the Prime Minister's attitude was pragmatic and legalistic. For him, no new principles were involved in increasing the Maynooth grant, either religious or constitutional. Though it was true that he was open to the charge of inconsistency — since he now supported what he and his party had opposed under the Whigs — even personal consistency, Peel believed, must give way before the menace to the United Kingdom involved in O'Connell's Repeal Movement of 1843 — an argument exactly similar to that employed by the Duke of Wellington in 1828–29! A conciliatory policy in Ireland was absolutely essential, and educational reform was an important part of that process. As *Punch* commented sardonically:

'How wonderful is Peel
He changes with the time . . .
He gives whate'er they want
To those who ask with zeal
He yields the Maynooth Grant
To the clamour for Repeal' (**121**).

Such a considered approach was unlikely to cut much ice with Peel's more rabid followers or those who had old scores to settle. For some Evangelicals, like Ashley, no truck with the Roman Catholic Church was to be tolerated. 'What a strange ignorance, or haughty contempt of the deep solemn Protestant feeling in the hearts of the British people', was his comment on Peel's proposal (**56**). More representative was the attitude of Anglicans such as Inglis, who resented being expected to vote for funds for Maynooth when the Church of England was denied grants for church extension. Maynooth represented, he argued, 'the endowment of the Church of Rome', thus raising the spectre of 'concurrent endowment' (state support for all religious communities). As we saw earlier, one of the most effective speeches came from Disraeli, who made the Maynooth controversy the occasion for a bitter personal attack on Peel's 'cunning . . . and habitual perfidy'. Indeed, the longer the debate went on in the spring of 1845 the more it became an inquest into Peel's personal integrity in relation to the Church of England, in 1829 and later.

Peel tried to convince himself that much of his backbenchers' opposition to the Maynooth Bill was the product of self-interest rather than religious concern. 'Tariff, drought, 46*s* a quarter for wheat, quicken the religious apprehensions of some; disappointed ambition, and the rejection of applications for office, of others', he wrote to Croker (**10**, iii). It is true that many agriculturalists opposed the Bill, and undoubtedly some of this opposition was an expression of their distaste for Peel's economic policies which, as the 1845 Budget showed, advanced even further in the direction of free trade. As a Dorset MP protested: 'it gave everything to the manufacturing and commercial interest and did nothing for the agricultural' (**16**). But it would be foolish to pretend that the 150 or so Conservative votes cast against Maynooth represented mere self-interest. They expressed much popular opinion in the country, as the national outcry against the government's proposals revealed (**66**). Maynooth also emphasised what earlier anti-government votes had suggested, that there was growing opposition among an important section of Tory backbenchers to Peel's leadership and to the direction in which he was taking the party. Peel became the target for their frustration over the position of agriculture, the changed role of the Church of England, and the difficulties of governing Ireland.

The Maynooth Bill in fact passed easily through the House of Commons in May 1845, owing to strong support from the Whigs and Irish. The Conservative Party was closely divided on the issue — 159 to 147 votes in favour on the second reading, and 149 to 148 against on the third reading. In the Lords too, though the Bill passed with a comfortable majority owing to the support of the Whig peers, the debates showed 'what a wide gap existed between the conservative leaders and many of their followers in the upper house' (**53**). The consequences of Maynooth were almost fatal for the party. Peel was determined to get the Bill through, and seems to have accepted with reckless abandon the inevitable personal unpopularity and loss of confidence among the party rank-and-file that was bound to follow. Graham was more bitter. 'The bill will pass but our party is destroyed', he wrote to a colleague. 'We have lost the slight hold which we ever possessed over the hearts and kind feelings of our followers' (**81**). In a letter to J. W. Croker he spelt out in impassioned detail the consequences for the party of what he regarded as the ingratitude of the country gentry [**doc. 20**]. Gash comes to a similar verdict on Maynooth. 'It was this episode', he writes, 'more than anything else, that finally destroyed the morale of the party and broke the last emotional tie between Peel and many of his followers' (**113**).

The final rupture was not to come yet. After the mounting tension of Maynooth, a period of torpor and anticlimax followed. The hard facts of political life — Tory hatred of the Whigs, the lack of an alternative Conservative leader, the personal influence of the Prime Minister — reasserted themselves and kept Peel in office. As Greville commented after the Maynooth Bill passed the Commons: 'Everybody expects that he means to go on, and in the end to knock the Corn Laws on the head, and endow the R.C. Church; but nobody knows how or when he will do these things' (**12**, v). As far as the Corn Laws were concerned the country did not have that long to wait.

Part Two: The Break-Up of the Conservative Party

5 The Corn Laws Crisis

The prospect of widespread famine in Ireland as a result of the potato-blight in October 1845 faced the Conservative government with the most serious crisis of its career. Suddenly, and for the grimmest possible reasons, the future of the Corn Laws was again thrust into the centre of the political stage; and this was bound to reactivate the whole problem of Peel's relations with the Conservative agriculturalists. Peel's immediate task was to determine a policy towards Ireland, and win over the Cabinet to it. He had no doubt what, in the circumstances, that policy must be. As early as 15 October he wrote to the Lord Lieutenant of Ireland: 'The accounts of the potato crop are very alarming . . . The remedy is the total and absolute repeal for ever of all duties on all articles of subsistence' (8, ii). Peel elaborated the problems involved in grappling with a possible Irish famine in a detailed and more tentative memorandum presented to the Cabinet on 1 November [doc. 21a].

At that and subsequent meetings during November it became clear that there were serious divisions within the Cabinet. Only three members (Graham, Aberdeen and Herbert) definitely supported the Prime Minister's proposals: to suspend the duties on grain immediately by an Order in Council; summon Parliament at the end of the month; and indicate that the government would later bring forward a Bill to modify the existing Corn Law. The rest of the Cabinet were either unconvinced that the situation in Ireland was as bad as Peel made out, or they were worried by the moral and political implications of a Conservative administration hitherto committed to agricultural protection supporting suspension and repeal. As Goulburn charged Peel, would not the public in those circumstances 'tax us with treachery and deception'; and would not the break-up of the Conservative Party that would surely follow repeal lead to 'the ultimate triumph of unrestrained democracy'? (8, ii). Despite sharp differences of opinion, all the members of the Cabinet expressed their confidence in the Prime Minister. But Peel was determined to resign unless he could obtain the full support of his colleagues, since he believed that without their backing the task of winning over the Conservative party to his proposals would be hopeless.

On 22 November, in his *Edinburgh Letter*, Lord John Russell, the Whig leader, announced his conversion to total repeal of the Corn Laws, a step which helped to polarise opinion within Parliament and the country and gave an enormous fillip to the Anti-Corn Law League. Three days later the Cabinet met again, and as the food situation in Ireland was clearly deteriorating, agreed to special relief measures there and to the secret import of maize from America. Peel now took a tougher line. He insisted that these actions must be accompanied by agreement to abandon the Corn Laws. He followed this up by a further series of powerful memoranda, in which inch by inch, by the sheer weight of his authority and powers of argument, he won over the majority of his colleagues to his programme of a progressive reduction in the corn duties until they were finally extinguished: immediate suspension was to be abandoned. This *volte-face* by the Cabinet was a remarkable tribute to Peel's leadership and persistence. It drives home the point that, as Gash suggests, there was no great commitment in principle to the Corn Laws within the Cabinet. 'The debate seemed to revolve for the most part around the time, mode, justification and responsibility of abandoning them' (**81**).

Nevertheless, Stanley and Buccleuch (Lord Privy Seal) still held out against the majority. On 5 December, therefore, Peel resigned. Russell tried, unsuccessfully, to form a government; and then handed back the responsibility to Peel who on 20 December resumed office as Prime Minister. For the Cabinet the issue was now no longer the problem of the Corn Laws, but rather that of carrying on the Queen's government effectively. As Wellington had insisted from the start: 'A good Government for the country is more important than Corn Laws or any other consideration', and that implied standing by Peel (**8**, ii). In these new circumstances even Buccleuch abandoned his opposition, and in the end only Stanley resigned, to be replaced as Colonial Secretary by Gladstone. Stanley's attitude was personal and quixotic: he was not prepared to oppose Peel publicly, but neither was he prepared to remain in the government, even though the preservation of party unity was — and had been since 1841 — his major political aim. 'It is no use arguing the matter', was his characteristic comment on Repeal. 'We cannot do this as gentlemen' (**127**).

With a united Cabinet behind him, Peel was now faced with the much more formidable task of obtaining a majority in the House of Commons for the repeal of the Corn Laws without antagonising the bulk of his Conservative supporters. In a series of six great speeches (between 22 January and 15 May 1846) Peel introduced, explained and defended his policy in detail. In his opening speeches in January he described his reasons for his change of heart over the Corn Laws, and put forward his specific proposals for repeal: a *gradual* reduction of duties down to 1849 (a deliberate attempt by Peel to win over moderate opinion), accompanied by a general programme of tariff reform and compensation for the agriculturalists. The Prime Minister found himself faced with the defection of two-thirds of his party, led by Lord George Bentinck — hitherto an obscure country gentleman, renowned more for his victories on the Turf than in the Commons — who proceeded to organise a Protectionist Party in opposition to the government.

Faced by defection and bitter personal attacks from men like Bentinck, Miles, Stafford O'Brien and — more viciously — Disraeli, Peel's later speeches were sharper and more uncompromising. It was clear that, given the strong support he received from Russell and Cobden, the Repeal Bill was bound to pass, whatever the consequences for the Conservative Party. In fact, on the final vote on 15 May, the government eventually obtained a majority of ninety-eight in favour of the repeal of the Corn Laws. On the other hand, 241 Conservatives voted against and only 112 for the Bill. In the following month, despite Bentinck's schemes and hopes, the Lords too fell into line with a majority of forty-seven in favour, largely owing to the discipline imposed on the Whig peers by Lord John Russell. In the end, therefore, the Repeal Act passed easily through Parliament, and was accepted without any great fuss by the country at large. The Corn Laws crisis was thus not really a national crisis, but one within the body of the Conservative Party itself.

For Peel victory over the Corn Laws was only achieved — as he eventually came to accept — at the price of his own political career. Once it became clear after the successful second reading in March that repeal would pass, then his power depended on the sufferance of the Whigs and the other anti-government groups in the House of Commons. And Bentinck was determined on revenge, even if it meant allying with the Whigs to destroy the Prime Minister. His chance came with the introduction of the Irish Coercion Bill. A few hours after the Lords agreed to the repeal of the Corn Laws on 26 June, the government was defeated in the Commons on the Irish

Bill by a 'blackguard combination' (as Wellington termed it) of Whigs, Radicals, Irish and Protectionists. On the following day Peel resigned as Prime Minister. He was never to hold office again.

Why then did Peel decide to support the repeal of the Corn Laws so quickly and determinedly in November to December 1845? It was not as if such actions could have a dramatic effect on the food supply in Ireland, given the fact that the Irish peasantry just could not afford to buy grain, and supplies from Europe were in any case limited (**18**). For Peel, opening the ports was in the first place a moral gesture, and part and parcel of his policy of conciliation in Ireland. To maintain the Corn Laws while Irishmen starved would be intolerable. Furthermore he had convinced himself that, given the state of public opinion, once suspended it would be impossible to re-impose the Corn Laws without a political furore which he was determined to avoid. In all this Peel was doubtless sincere. But it is also important to realise that by late 1845 he no longer had any faith in the Corn Laws and was unprepared to go on defending them. Indeed, it has been argued that as early as 1841−42 Peel had abandoned any real intellectual conviction in their favour (**118**). He sympathised with Graham's view, expressed in a letter to him at the time of the 1842 Corn Bill:

> 'In truth, it is a question of *time*. The next change in the Corn Laws must be to an open trade; and if our population increase for two or three years at the rate of 300,000 per annum, you may throw open the ports, and British agriculture will not suffer. But the next change must be the last; it is not prudent to hurry it; next session is too soon.' (**10**, iii)

As a memorandum of the Prince Consort shows, Peel seems to have envisaged 'educating his party' *before* the next election, and winning their support for repeal so that a united Conservative Party could then face the electorate in 1847 [**doc. 21b**]. It was the onset of the crisis in Ireland that forced him to act precipitately. But it was a step that, psychologically, he was predisposed to take. It meant for him the removal of the heavy burden of divided loyalties over the Corn Laws, between private belief and public profession. It would also enable him to dispose of the question once and for all − which in itself would be a remarkable political coup − and for the best of humanitarian motives.

Peel abandoned support for the Corn Laws largely for economic reasons. By the end of 1845 he was convinced that the progress of the nation showed the soundness of free trade policy.

'Does not the state of the revenue (he wrote to a Conservative supporter in the New Year) buoyant under all our reductions, the state of commerce and manufacture, above all, the spirit of contentment and loyalty for the last three years, speak volumes in favour of the continued application — to articles of manufacture as well as to the produce of the land — of those principles, the caution and deliberate adoption of which has mainly led to our present prosperity?' (**10**, iii)

These hard facts, together with his new intellectual conviction that reduced wages need not follow lower wheat prices, led him to argue that there was no good reason why agriculture, like other branches of the economy, should not be subject to the laws of *laissez-faire*. Indeed, the encouragement of sound enterprise and healthy competition by the removal of protective barriers would stimulate agricultural productivity and efficiency. This last point was particularly important for Peel, for what gave a sharper edge to his economic thinking were his fears for the sources of British wheat supply abroad and the need to encourage home wheat production in an age of rising population, though these were not points he emphasised in the debates in the House of Commons, where he was anxious to widen support by stressing the 'moral' argument (**18**). This underlines the point that for Peel the key economic issue in the Corn Laws debates was not really the fate of Ireland, but rather the condition of life of the British masses; the theme of the great peroration at the end of his resignation speech on 29 June 1846 [**doc. 23**].

In advancing these reasons for repeal, 'Peel did not believe that he was undermining 'true Conservatism' or acting inconsistently. He had never supported the Corn Laws in principle, nor did he believe that their defence should be a *sine qua non* of Conservative policy. He accepted, however, that a commitment to agricultural protection was widespread within the Conservative Party, and that he himself had tacitly accepted it in 1841—42. Yet he argued vigorously and repeatedly that in crisis situations, party interest — even personal consistency — must give way to national interest. 'When I do fall, I shall have the satisfaction of reflecting that I do not fall because I preferred the interests of party to the general interests of the community' (**11**, iv). Moreover, it was the duty of the Prime Minister to decide what that 'national interest' was. He was determined, said Peel, to hold office 'by no servile tenure. I will only hold that office upon the condition of being unshackled by any other obligations than those of consulting the public interest, and of providing for the public safety' (**11**, iv).

Even from the point of view of Conservative political interests, Peel believed that it was misguided to cling to a policy of agricultural protection. To link the defence of the aristocratic order with a dogmatic commitment to the Corn Laws was futile and short-sighted, and could prove disastrous. Economically, the interests of agriculture were intertwined with those of manufacture and commerce, and all three would benefit from free trade. Politically, the retention of the Corn Laws rendered the landed interest particularly vulnerable to attack since, as a Tory aristocrat admitted to Peel, 'they are considered as a class monopoly' (**10**, iii). Hence, as the Prime Minister insisted vehemently: 'I trust that a territorial aristocracy . . . will long be maintained. I believe such an aristocracy to be essential to the purposes of good government . . . The question is at present, will the legitimate influence of the landed aristocracy be better maintained by consenting to forego this protection or insisting upon the maintenance of it?' (**11**, iv). Peel had no doubt that the former was the case. Hence what he was trying to do in 1846 was what he had been aiming at since 1832: to persuade the Conservative Party to adapt itself to a changed social and economic environment, and thus save the landed interest from the consequences of its own folly. He aimed to strengthen rather than diminish the influence of the established ruling class. Politically, his differences with the Protectionists were over means, not ends.

Peel's perspective in viewing the crisis of 1845–46 was therefore as much political as economic. The Corn Laws were a divisive element in British society. Repeal was vital, therefore, in order 'to terminate a conflict which, according to our belief, would soon place in hostile collision great and powerful classes in the community', a conflict which, as in 1831–32, the aristocracy might lose (**11**, iv). Retreat was necessary for the defenders of the Corn Laws. But it was to be an orderly retreat, controlled, step by step, by the Prime Minister *within* Parliament, and not as the result of an electoral contest in which the complex issues of free trade and protection would be bandied about at the hustings and the very foundations of the established political system would be under attack (**52**). Nor was he prepared to yield to Radical 'pressure from without'; particularly pressure from the Anti-Corn Law League, now (according to Graham) 'the most formidable movement in modern times' (**10**, iii). In fact Peel's parliamentary strategy meant that the League was rendered isolated and impotent during the Corn Laws crisis, the spectator rather than the creator of events. These tactics, Peel believed, would enable the forces of the landed interest to regroup in good order again once the Corn Laws had been abandoned.

It is these political aims that help to explain the alacrity with which Peel took up the cause of repeal in November 1845, and his refusal to ask for a dissolution and an election after his resignation on 5 December. His attitude at the time of his final resignation in June 1846 was the same. He was loath to fight an election which would turn so much on his own reputation and conduct, and where his followers would be allied with the Anti-Corn Law League in 'an unnatural combination with those who agree with us in nothing but the principles of Free Trade' (**10**, iii). Besides, his major tasks had now been accomplished. He was anxious to free himself from the 'intolerable burden' of office and the curse of 'party attachment' [**doc. 24a**].

Peel's arguments had little effect on the Tory agriculturalists and their supporters. In the first place they were sceptical about the extent of famine in Ireland; and many of them believed that Ireland was merely an excuse for Peel's long-premeditated plan to destroy the Corn Laws, for which there was no economic justification. The 1842 Corn Law was working well, prices were relatively stable, farmers and labourers were prospering — what need was there for repeal? Nor were they impressed by Peel's arguments in favour of 'High Farming' as a substitute for protection: farmers could only afford improvements if protection was maintained, and the grants suggested in the proposed Bill were derisory. Repeal would mean the ruination of British agriculture.

But economic arguments, which neither side really explored in depth, were not the most important part of the protectionists' case. Their real justification was political, perhaps psychological. They were concerned with the more imponderable consequences of repeal: with questions of personal honour and consistency, party loyalty and party principles. For a Conservative stateman to carry repeal was to connive with the Anti-Corn Law League — the symbol of popular agitation and organisation — in a major step towards democracy. 'If the Anti-Corn Law League succeed in ruining the Agricultural interest', said the Duke of Richmond, addressing his fellow agriculturalists, 'I will ask you whether they will stop there . . . It is the first step: they feel that it is the yeomanry of England that stand between them and the democratic principles which they wish to carry out' (**128**). Repeal meant betraying those classes who looked towards the Conservative Party for support. 'Questions of prices of corn and rates of wages', wrote J. W. Croker, 'are mere *accidents*; the *substance* is the existence of a landed gentry, which has made England what she has been and is' (**7**, iii).

This theme of 'betrayal', already implicit in Stanley's resignation from the Cabinet, is at the heart of the protectionists' attack on Peel. The Conservative Party had been elected and Peel had become Prime Minister in 1841 on the basis of public support for the Corn Laws. Yet three years after his revised Corn Law of 1842 he was pushing through a Bill for total repeal without any consultation with his followers — a typical example of Peelite tyranny, arrogance and double-dealing! As Bentinck himself was supposed to have said: 'I keep horses in three counties, and they tell me that I shall save fifteen hundred a year by free trade. I don't care for that: what I cannot bear is being *sold*' (**74**). Peel claimed to be defending a higher 'national interest'. But who could determine what *was* the national interest? Far better for the ordinary Tory MP to cleave to what he knew: party interest and party principles. In a stinging attack on Peel, Disraeli argued that this was the bedrock of parliamentary government [**doc. 24b**].

Whatever the merits of the protectionists' case, as we have seen it had no effect on the passage into law of the government's Repeal Act. The real importance of the Conservative attack on Peel in 1846 lies in the fact that it led to the formation of the Protectionist Party, an outcome which was unexpected for both the Prime Minister and most MPs. The impetus for this move came originally not from within the House of Commons, but from outside, particularly among the farmers who were associated with local Protection Societies and membership of the Central Agricultural Protection Society, the Anti-League. The Anti-League, which had been formed in 1844, had had little success in combating the formidable propaganda of the Anti-Corn Law League, mainly because the gentry and aristocrats in its leadership had strong inhibitions about employing the radical methods of the League to advance the Protectionist cause. Moreover its rules forbade it interfering in party politics, nor was its influence on the Commons very great. There the farmers were personally unrepresented, and the landowners who sat for the shires and small rural boroughs, though they had long-standing grievances against Peel, were reluctant to weaken a Conservative administration seriously even if they had possessed the leadership and ability to do so. In the later months of 1845 it looked as if Peel's plans for repeal had little to fear from the rank-and-file of Tory MPs (**64**).

By the end of the year, however, worried by rumours of Peel's intentions over the Corn Laws, the farmers were impatient for action [**doc. 25**]. After the Prime Minister's resignation and return to office in December, they began to organise meetings and petitions on a wide scale, throughout the southern counties especially, in defence of protection. 'The Agricultural Constituencies', wrote Bentinck to his father on 2 January, 'seem to be riding in every direction, and the cry of "No Surrender" seems very general' (**127**). What this meant was that to a considerable extent it was the tenant farmers who took over control of the resistance movement in the counties. It was they rather than the landowners who were most belligerent in their opposition to Peel (**35**). The 'no politics' rule was rescinded by the Anti-League; and the farmers began to tighten the screw on their more cautious representatives in the House of Commons to ensure that they continued the parliamentary struggle against repeal and ultimately voted as their constituents expected. It was a pressure that most of the agriculturalist MPs found difficult to resist.

It was the farmers then who did most of the original spadework in the countryside in the winter of 1845–46 that enabled a Protectionist Party to emerge in the House of Commons (**54**). By the spring of 1846 it was well on the way to becoming a third party force. It had its own leaders, notably Bentinck, who by sheer force of will and conviction turned the Protectionist opposition to the government 'from a protest into a rebellion' (**128**). It possessed national support, its own organisation and finances (Bonham and the Whips supported Peel), and a clear-cut policy of opposition to repeal at any price. It was Bentinck who helped to organise the anti-government vote in Parliament, in collaboration with men such as Miles, O'Brien, Disraeli, and the Duke of Buckingham, and established close relations with the Anti-League. Stanley remained aloof from these activities, though he became *de facto* leader of the Protectionist Party in the Lords. Outside Parliament, in the constituencies, the Protectionists worked with great effect to prevent the return of Conservative free-traders. Gladstone, for example, to his own and the government's embarrassment, after his appointment as Colonial Secretary, found it difficult to find a safe seat when he stood for re-election, and was therefore out of the Commons during the crucial debates. Lords Lincoln and Ashley were both defeated in by-elections by Protectionists. All this had a decisive effect on the Conservative Party. Despite his success in guiding the Repeal Bill through the House of Commons, Peel found, for the first time, that control of the Conservative Party was slipping out of his hands.

These developments help us to understand the character of the final vote on the Repeal Bill on 15 May 1846: the government obtained a majority of ninety-eight, but 241 Conservatives voted against the Bill and only 112 in favour. How are we to account for these Tory figures? It has been shown that it is virtually impossible to differentiate between the pro- and anti-groups in terms of status, background or income — the landowning classes were represented on both sides (**27**). Yet though the Conservative supporters and opponents of repeal may not differ much in terms of their standing as individual MPs, they differ markedly when looked at from the point of view of their constituencies. 86 per cent of Conservatives representing the counties and universities voted against repeal; so did 63 per cent of those who sat for small rural boroughs (**113, 35**). This is clearly a reflection of the strength of agricultural opinion on the issue; and indeed we know that some MPs (Lord John Manners, for example) were prepared to bow to the wishes of their constituents and vote against the government, even though they were personally free-traders.

But the anti-government vote of 15 May is also closely related to the similar votes that had preceded it. 'The disruption of 1846 was not a sudden unpredictable event, but the culmination of a long period of intensifying strain' (**113**). It is no coincidence that out of the 150 Conservatives who voted against the Maynooth Bill in May 1845, 135 also voted against repeal a year later. In similar fashion, many of those who voted for Peel in May 1846 did so — whether they were committed free-traders or not — because they were either associated with the governing elite, or believed that the retention of a strong Conservative administration should override all other considerations.

To some extent the enormous Conservative anti-government vote of 15 May 1846 was an exceptional incident — the outcome of special circumstances, emotions and influences. This is revealed by the subsequent vote on the Irish Coercion Bill on 25 June, which was largely immune from outside pressure now that repeal was a *fait accompli*. Out of the 112 MPs who had supported Peel over the Corn Laws, 110 voted with him again; but of the 241 Protectionists, 116 now voted for the government, 74 voted against, while 51 abstained (**27**). Thus about one-third of those Protectionists who had opposed Peel on 15 May supported him on 25 June. This is perhaps a reflection of their unease at the revengeful animosity displayed by

Bentinck and Disraeli towards the Prime Minister, and their longing for Conservative unity. It is also an expression of the genuine support of many Tory backbenchers for the Bill and apprehension at the prospect of a Whig administration. But their pro-government vote was now merely a nostalgic gesture. More important was the fact that 125 Conservatives refused to support the government's Irish Bill with their votes, and were prepared to accept, indeed welcome, the inevitable destruction of the ministry that followed. It was the vote on 25 June that revealed the true strength of the Protectionist Party in the House of Commons, and marked the end of Peel's leadership of a united Conservative Party [**doc. 22**].

For this disruption Peel bears a heavy responsibility. 'From the language he held to me in December 1845', wrote Gladstone in old age, 'I think he expected to carry the repeal of the Corn Laws without breaking up his party. But meant at all hazards to carry it' (**4**, iii). From the start Peel refused to consider any compromise between the 1842 Corn Law and total repeal; and in the end his pride and sense of rectitude made him widen rather than narrow the gap between himself and his opponents. His eulogy on Richard Cobden, for example, in his resignation speech on 29 June, outraged the Protectionists, and placed his own followers in an uncomfortable position. Similarly, though he had his reasons, he refused to meet the Conservative backbenchers to discuss repeal, or to involve the public through a general election. His 'high' conception of the Prime Minister's office, which during the crisis seemed almost to degenerate into a demand for blind obedience from the Tory rank-and-file, made things worse, especially as it seemed based upon a rejection of the very party system which had given him power. 'As heads see and tails are blind, I think heads are the best judges as to the course to be taken', he later commented (**10**, iii). Disraeli was not being wholly unfair, therefore, when he wrote of. Peel in December 1845: 'He is so vain that he wants to figure in history as the settler of all great questions; but a Parliamentary constitution is not favourable to such ambitions: things must be done by parties not by persons using parties as tools . . .' (**127**).

What all this meant was that Peel conspicuously lacked the political tact and flexibility, the intuitive understanding of his followers that would inspire their trust and affection and allow them to follow him down an unfamiliar and hazardous path. 'In my judgement', wrote a sympathetic backbencher of Peel's action in 1846, 'no charge of treachery can be maintained, and the change of opinion was honest. But we may regret that Sir Robert had not taken his supporters sooner into his confidence and "educated" his party' (**113**).

From a wider point of view, however, the consequences of the Corn Laws crisis to a large extent justified Peel's hopes. Economically, the demise of the Corn Laws was followed not by ruin for the agriculturalists, but by increased rent rolls and farming profits based on rising population and expanding demand for British produce. This itself was a reflection of the genuine rise in living standards of the working classes in the mid-nineteenth century. Nor, as Peel had hoped, did 1846 mark the end of aristocratic influence. Despite its own internal divisions on the issue, the landed interest in the end accepted the wisdom of repeal deliberately and advisedly; by doing so its members maintained their own unity and right to govern. Indeed, by ending the Corn Law question once and for all – and with it the *raison d'être* of the Anti-Corn Law League – they helped to restore their own pre-eminence. In that sense repeal was not a defeat for the landed interest, as has often been supposed. Nor, for Peel, was it intended to be. For him, 'Repeal was a strategic retreat, the sacrifice of the bastion of the Corn Laws in order to keep intact the main stronghold of aristocratic power' (**15**). That, he believed, he had secured. 'It is my firm persuasion', he told his Tamworth constituents in July 1847, 'that our commercial and financial policy . . . has tended to fortify the established institutions of the country . . . to maintain the just authority of an hereditary nobility, and to discourage the desire for democratic change in the constitution of the House of Commons' (**52**). As the history of the next twenty years showed, it was a reasonable verdict.

6 Peel and the Peelites

After the repeal of the Corn Laws Peel occupied a unique position in the country as the greatest statesman of the age, virtually 'above politics'; and, until his death in 1850, he dominated the House of Commons. During these four years Peel was determined never again to seek office or to become the leader of a party, though he fully intended to play a vigorous role as an MP (**10**, iii). His attitude was well described by Graham (as reported by Greville):

> 'Peel's position is a very extraordinary one and he is determined to enjoy it. He has an immense fortune, is in full possession of his faculties and vigour, has great influence and consideration in Parliament and the country . . . In this position he will not retire from public life to please any man; he does not want to be head of a party, still less to return to office, but he will continue to take that part in public affairs which he considers best for the public service.' (**12**, v)

Peel's main aim now was to ensure that no attempt was made by his successors to return to a policy of agricultural protection; and he was prepared, therefore, to go to almost any lengths to maintain the Whig government in power and keep it on the right Peelite path. This meant supporting it against the Protectionists and, when necessary, its own Radical left wing.

Peel was therefore generally prepared to go along with Whig policy during the early years of Russell's ministry, even when it went against the grain. He supported the government over Ireland and acquiesced in its policies of social reform. He came to the ministry's rescue in 1847 when the Bank of England was attacked by Protectionists, and supported them in the following year over the Budget and the income tax against both Protectionists and Radical critics. In 1849 he did his best, behind the scenes, to win support among his followers for the government's proposed repeal of the Navigation Laws, which in the end passed with a handsome majority. Peel's advice and sympathy were welcomed by the Whig ministers, particularly Sir Charles Wood, the Chancellor of the

Exchequer, who became virtually Peel's protégé at the Treasury. Almost the only occasion when Peel spoke out directly against the Whig ministry was his attack on Palmerston in 1850 over the Don Pacifico affair, when he found himself on the same side as Gladstone, Disraeli and Cobden; and then he was confident, correctly as it turned out, that the government would not be imperilled by his action.

Yet by attempting to act as an independent member of the House of Commons, Peel was not only deluding himself — 'he *must* be a leader in spite of himself', as Stanley remarked — he also placed his followers, the famous '112' who had voted with him in favour of repeal, in an impossible position. He refused to support even the most tentative attempts at Conservative reunion in 1846—47, though this was almost certainly a forlorn hope while Bentinck led the Protectionists in the Commons. But neither was he prepared to encourage any positive moves towards the Whig camp, despite his benevolent attitude towards the government. As it was, many of the leading Peelites thought he was too subservient to the Russell ministry; they were prepared on occasion to use their votes in their own way, and none of them were willing to rise to Russell's bait when he dangled the prospect of major government posts before them. Moreover, Peel eschewed even the slightest attempt to organise his followers into a party, or encourage anyone else to do so, despite prodding from Bonham and Sir John Young, the Chief Whip. He even expressed a lack of interest in the results of the 1847 general election. This negative attitude bewildered and irritated even his most loyal disciples, especially Gladstone, who wrote some years later of Peel's 'thoroughly false position for the last four years of his life'. Peel thus contributed decisively during this period to the confusions and uncertainties of political life, and 'kept the party system in a state of suspended animation' (**101**).

Nevertheless, despite the problems that faced them, the Peelites did rather better in the general election of 1847 than many had expected. They kept up their numbers, and all their leading ex-ministers were returned to the Commons. That election was inevitably a muddled affair owing to the disintegration of the two-party system — 'a battle of causes rather than of parties' (**46**) — and the major cause was Protestantism rather than protection, since the Maynooth issue was rekindled by Peel in his election address. Most candidates in fact attuned their message to the interests of their constituents.

The Times estimated that there were 336 Liberals (as the Whigs and Radicals were now often called) returned; 201 Protectionists; and 117 Peelites – a verdict which represented a clear rebuff to Bentinck and Stanley. But in detail these figures mean very little owing to the obvious difficulties in accurately classifying the political allegiance of MPs. In particular, the *Times* figure for the Peelites is almost certainly too high, since not all free-trade Conservatives can be regarded as true Peelites – men such as Aberdeen, Graham and Gladstone, who were tied to Sir Robert by bonds of intellectual conviction and personal loyalty, and who were unprepared to support an overtly Protectionist administration. As Stanley observed cynically of the electoral results, 'on all sides there will be a great number of loose fish' (**120**); and much turned on the way in which MPs used their votes in the parliamentary divisions.

What is clear is that the Peelites suffered after the 1847 election from their lack of leadership and cohesion. As Gladstone observed despondently in 1849: 'We have no party, no organisation, no whipper-in; and under these circumstances we cannot exercise any considerable degree of permanent influence as a body' (**89**, i). This was reflected in a continuous decline in their numbers; and divisions within the hard core of Peelites who remained over both tactics and policy. Over such key issues as the Ten Hours Bill, the Sugar Duties and Jewish Disabilities, for example, the Peelites were split down the middle. 'What are we to do', Goulburn lamented, 'who cannot approve of the acts of the Government on the one hand nor of the acts and opinions of Lord G. Bentinck or D'Israeli on the other?' (**101**). It was a question which still remained unresolved when Peel himself died, tragically, on 2 July 1850 as the result of a riding accident.

The death of Sir Robert Peel was mourned by the whole country, particularly by the working classes [**doc. 26**] (**123**). It had no dramatic effect, however, on parliamentary politics or the position of the Peelites. The latter were now reduced to between sixty and seventy members; and they still possessed no real leader. Lord Aberdeen, who in terms of character and experience was the most obvious candidate for that position, was reluctant to push himself forward; and the younger men, though they made some effort at organising the Peelite forces, were preoccupied with other matters – Gladstone, for example, was absent in Italy from 1850 to 1851. Nor were the Peelites any more united now in their attitudes towards the two great blocs of Whigs and Conservatives in the House of Commons. As *The Times* commented, not unfairly: 'Their present difficulty is that they are not a party; they have not its ties; they have not its facilities; they have not its obligations'. All that ties them together is 'a mere historical connexion with Sir Robert Peel' (**102**). Nevertheless, both Russell and Stanley continued to court them, since though the Peelite numbers declined rapidly after the death of Sir Robert, the zeal and ability of their leaders — particularly Gladstone, Herbert and Cardwell — were obvious to all, and they would provide a considerable catch for any Whig or Protectionist administration.

One result of Peel's death, however, was to make his followers more independent of the Whigs; and this was emphasised by the impact of yet another religious crisis, the so-called 'Papal Aggression' of 1851. In the autumn of the previous year the Pope had taken steps to restore the Roman Catholic episcopate in England, and this was announced to the faithful by Cardinal Wiseman in his notorious pastoral letter, 'Out of the Flaminian Gate'. The ambiguity and extravagance of Wiseman's language helped to re-awaken the anti-popish prejudices of English Protestantism, already alarmed by the growth of High-Church sentiments within the Church of England. This led to a violent campaign against the Church of Rome, even more virulent than that over Maynooth five years earlier (**66**). What was singular about the present outburst was that Lord John Russell, the Prime Minister, gave it his stamp of approval, mainly in order to strengthen his tottering government by giving it a populist flavour — yet another example of his extraordinary political unpredictability. His Ecclesiastical Titles Bill, which banned the use of all Roman Catholic ecclesiastical titles throughout the United Kingdom, was introduced into the House of Commons in February 1851 and passed by 395 votes to sixty-three. The most distinguished opposition to the Bill came from the Peelite leaders in both Houses, who were united in defence of religious liberty, a stand which at least won them the gratitude and later support of the Irish group in the House of Commons.

It was this religious issue above all which led to a growing coolness between the Peelites and the Whigs, though there were of course traditional antipathies on both sides. Graham, for example, the most pro-Whig of the Peelite leaders (he had served under Melbourne in the 1830s), refused the offer of the Home Secretaryship from Russell. When the latter was defeated in the Commons on 20 February over the Franchise Bill, as the result of a Radical revolt, it proved impossible to bring Russell, Aberdeen and their political friends together to discuss the formation of a coalition government, despite the efforts of the Queen and Prince Albert. Stanley's half-hearted attempt to form a ministry also failed. As the Queen commented, with some irritation, on the constitutional crisis: 'The "Papal Question" is the real and almost insuperable difficulty, and next to it, the question of free trade' (**66**). Russell therefore returned to office — but not to power — only to be ousted for a second time, at the hands of Lord Palmerston, almost exactly one year later in February 1852. This was Pam's famous 'tit-for-tat' for his own dismissal from the Whig government in the previous December, following his premature recognition as Foreign Secretary of the *coup d'état* of Louis Napoleon. Though they intensely disliked his foreign policy, Palmerston's action was supported by most of the Peelite leaders, now weary of Lord John's impetuousness and incompetence.

The relations between the Peelites and the Protectionists were inevitably more sensitive than with the Whigs. If Conservative reunion was virtually hopeless while Bentinck led the Protectionists in the Commons, even after his death in 1848 and that of Peel two years later, the efforts of Stanley to entice back the Peelite leaders proved unavailing. The question of free trade still remained a major stumbling block; but there were also more subtle differences of ideas and outlook, and clashes of personality, which still persisted. In attempting to form a government in February 1851 after the first resignation of Russell, Stanley offered Gladstone — just returned from Italy — virtually any post in his Cabinet. His friend and colleague, the Duke of Newcastle (formerly Lord Lincoln) urged him to refuse: 'I am sure our rule of conduct at this juncture, must be a prudent waiting on events . . .' (**102**). Though Gladstone, who was probably the most sympathetic to reunion of all the younger Peelites, was tempted, he rejected the offer, ostensibly on the grounds that Stanley was still committed to the restoration of a corn duty. One suspects that there were deeper forces at work, as Gladstone's conversion to religious freedom and recent support for Italian nationalism reveal (**92**). The upshot of all this was that the Earl of Derby (as Stanley had now become) abandoned any attempt to win over the Peelites, and went ahead and formed a purely Protectionist administration in March 1852, composed largely of unknown mediocrities, apart from Disraeli at the Treasury.

Now that a Conservative government was in office once more, the Peelites were forced to define their attitude towards their old party more precisely. Should they support or oppose Derby and Disraeli? Once again there was hesitancy and disagreement, as Gladstone indicated in his analysis of the situation [**doc. 27**]. 'My opinions went one way', he said, 'my lingering sympathies the other' (**89**, i); and he and his colleagues in the end plumped for a policy of 'wait and see'. They were prepared to give the Conservatives a fair trial until they committed themselves over free trade and finance. The general election that followed was therefore a dull affair: many seats were uncontested; issues were blurred; there was much corruption. The government, however, did reasonably well; and in the end there were some 300 Conservatives and about the same number of Liberals, with forty to fifty Peelites.

For the moment Derby continued as the leader of a minority government; but he was now clearly on trial and everything turned on his policies. Russell and Aberdeen were already disenchanted with the Conservatives because of their behaviour during the election, particularly their appeals to religious bigotry and inconsistency over free trade. Gladstone was soon incensed with Disraeli's 'unscrupulousness' in seeking votes in any quarter of the House to bolster the government (**102**). He was clearly spoiling for a fight with the new Chancellor of the Exchequer. His chance came when Disraeli introduced his Budget in early December 1852. It was a creditable performance by ordinary standards. But it infuriated Gladstone, since in its proposed relief for the landed classes and its revisions of the income tax it appeared to be undermining the principles of Peelite finance, and thus tarnished the memory of the great dead statesman. On the night of 16—17 December, in one of his greatest and most impassioned speeches, Gladstone tore Disraeli's Budget to shreds. It was a remarkable performance [**doc. 28**]. At one stroke it sealed the fate of the ministry: it also 'inaugurated the mythology of Gladstone as the great master of Victorian financial policy' (**92**). It did more. It determined the future of the Peelites, though no-one quite realised it at the time. It helped to destroy forever the possibility of their reunion with the Conservatives, and pushed Gladstone and his friends inexorably towards the Whigs. The government was defeated on the Budget by 305 to 286: out of the tiny group of Peelites who remained, thirty-five voted with the opposition and only five for the government. With the collapse of the first Derby administration, the weary process of carrying on the Queen's government began once again.

Everything pointed inescapably to a Whig-Peelite coalition. Since 1846 it had become clear that the tide of national opinion was running against the Conservatives. During the recent Derby ministry the Peelites had occupied the Opposition benches alongside the Whigs;

and there was growing sympathy between Russell and Aberdeen. The latter wrote to Graham that he was 'thoroughly convinced of the necessity of a Government of progress', though he added the caveat, '. . . but this progress must be Conservative in principle' (**75**). With their tiny numbers isolation was an increasingly dangerous position for the Peelites. Moreover, little now separated them from the Whigs over policy other than 'lingering political traditions that no longer had any great significance' (**102**). On the fundamental issue of financial and commercial policy they were in accord; they both supported religious freedom, despite Russell's aberration over 'Papal Aggression'; they both accepted the necessity of administrative reform and some extension of the franchise. In most respects Russell was now closer to the Peelites than the Radicals, who were anyway a declining force in the 1850s.

Newcastle put the position quite bluntly when he wrote to Aberdeen: 'Union with Lord Derby is impossible. Isolation is pleasant but not patriotic. Co-operation with other Liberals is requisite' (**72**). Not all Peelites agreed. Some, like Sir George Young, were alarmed at the prospect of abandoning the hope of a united Conservative party, and the fillip that this might give to 'the Radicals and the Irish Brass-band' (**102**). Gladstone too had earlier that year argued that union with the Whigs was the 'least natural position' for Peel's followers. Now, however, even he accepted that there seemed to be no real practical alternative, and the prospect of office again was particularly enticing.

But who was to lead a Whig-Peelite coalition? Russell accepted that, for the moment, he was ruled out as neither Peelites nor Palmerston would serve under him; nor would the Peelites accept Pam as Prime Minister. Lord Aberdeen became the inevitable choice; and he showed remarkable despatch and firmness in forming his government. The Cabinet he appointed at the end of December 1852 consisted of six Peelites — himself, Graham, Herbert, Newcastle, Argyle, and Gladstone at the Exchequer; six Whigs — including Palmerston at the Home Office and Russell as Foreign Secretary; and one nominal Radical. The Whigs dominated the non-Cabinet posts, though the Peelite Cardwell secured the Board of Trade. Given the fact that they numbered only about forty MPs, the Peelites did remarkably well in the distribution of offices, to the disgust of many Whigs; and this was a tribute to their prestige, leadership and ability — not to their influence in Parliament or the country. Indeed, the establishment of the Whig-Peelite coalition of 1852 was an almost eighteenth-century piece of Cabinet-making, accomplished by the governing elite with the approbation of the Crown (**72**). The balance of power within the Cabinet also reflected Aberdeen's deliberate intent. He did not want a coalition which represented the absorption of the Peelites into the Whig party; he aimed to create a new sort of ministry with a unity and purpose of its own, which could appeal to Whigs, Peelites *and* moderate Conservatives. 'The new government', he wrote, 'must not be a revival of the old Whig Cabinet with an addition of some Peelites, but should be a liberal Conservative government in the sense of Sir Robert Peel' (**39**).

On the domestic front at least that aspiration appeared to be well founded. The impulse for reform and administrative efficiency came largely from the Peelites. Gladstone's great Budget of 1853 was a deliberate and successful attempt to continue Peel's free trade policies [**doc. 28**]. It was the Peelites — and Gladstone especially — who enthusiastically supported the recommendations of the radical Northcote-Trevelyan Report of 1853 on civil service reform, compared with the lukewarm response of the Whigs. It was Gladstone too who was mainly responsible for the implementation of the Act of 1854 which reformed the archaic statutes of the University of Oxford. But other important proposals had to be shelved: a Parliamentary Reform Bill was abandoned owing to the international situation. 'The country is now bent on war', wrote Wood to Russell in February 1854, 'and will not trouble itself about reform' (**75**).

It was indeed daunting problems of foreign policy that overshadowed the government's domestic achievements and hopes after its first moderately successful year in office. In late 1853, rivalry between Russia and France over the guardianship of the Holy Places in Jerusalem, and increased pressure upon Turkey by Russia, forced Great Britain, the traditional defender of Turkish sovereignty, to intervene in the Near East. The Cabinet was divided over what attitude to adopt towards Russian pretensions. Aberdeen's placatory policy was supported by the Peelites; Palmerston on the other hand argued that a tougher policy towards Russia was necessary if war was to be avoided. Anxious to keep his government together, Aberdeen dithered — and the country gradually drifted into a war with Russia in defence of Turkey. The whole Cabinet in the end supported the declaration of war on Russia by Britain and France in March 1854, a war which was enormously popular in this country (**60**).

It was the stresses of the Crimean War that revealed some of the inherent weaknesses of the coalition government that had been papered over at its inception in 1852. These were largely the result (as Greville argued) of the very ability of the key figures in the Cabinet, whose ambitions and jealousies poisoned and eventually destroyed the ministry [**doc. 29**]. All this was brought to a head by the disasters of the first year of the war, and the sufferings of the troops at Sebastopol, for which, on the political side at least, Lord Aberdeen and his unimaginative War Minister, the Peelite Duke of Newcastle, were not unfairly blamed. The public soon clamoured for a scapegoat. On 23 January 1855 the Radical J. A. Roebuck introduced his famous motion into the House of Commons calling for the appointment of a Select Committee on the conduct of the war. That very evening Lord John Russell resigned. Russell's action disgusted his colleagues, and also the Queen, who in reply to his resignation letter curtly acknowledged his decision 'to desert the government' (**39**). When, a few days later, the Roebuck motion passed by 305 votes to 148, it was clear that the ministry had lost the confidence of the House of Commons, and Aberdeen resigned. As in May 1940, the country was now faced with a constitutional crisis in the midst of a major war.

Lacking the support of Palmerston, Derby realised it was hopeless to attempt to form a ministry; Russell was now outlawed by everyone; inevitably, therefore, Pam became Prime Minister, as he was the hero of the war party and the only man who could hope to win the favour of the Commons. 'Palmerston Prime Minister', commented John Bright, the anti-war Radical, 'what a hoax! The aged charlatan has at length attained the great object of his long and unscrupulous ambition' (**13**). Palmerston's ministry of February 1855 was the old coalition government minus Aberdeen, Newcastle and Russell. Gladstone and the remaining Peelite ministers − whose views on Pam were similar to Bright's − only continued in office reluctantly as a result of Aberdeen's pleas. But a few weeks later, when the Prime Minister supported the setting up of the Roebuck Committee, Gladstone, Herbert, Graham and Cardwell indignantly resigned, as a protest (in Gladstone's words) against 'the now chronic state of executive weakness' (**4**, iii). Only Argyle remained as the sole Peelite representative in what was now a Palmerstonian ministry.

The Whig-Peelite coalition, founded with such high hopes in December 1852, thus ended just over two years later in a flurry of resignations and recriminations. Yet it marked an important stage on the road to the united Liberal Party which emerged after 1859;

and for this Lord Aberdeen bears the major responsibility (**75, 102**). For the moment, however, the Peelites were in an unenviable position: they were a tiny group, out of office, isolated and unpopular. As Sidney Herbert had correctly foreseen, their resignation meant, as he told Aberdeen, that 'we shall draw down on ourselves all the indignation now resting on Lord John for selfishness and indifference to the public interests' (**93**, i). The Peelites' high-mindedness seemed to have taken them back to the sorry position they occupied before 1852. It is true that, confronted with difficult issues of war and peace, Palmerston's majority in the House of Commons was uncertain (**73**). But he was faced with a deeply fragmented opposition; and besides, Pam could hope to appeal to the public when the time was ripe over the heads of his political enemies in Parliament. That is exactly what did happen in the general election of 1857, after an apparently chastened Russia had signed the Peace of Paris in the previous year. It was a Palmerstonian triumph. Pam gained a majority of eighty-five; the anti-war Radicals were massacred, and the Peelites were reduced to a rump of twenty-five − basically the ex-Ministers of Peel's great ministry and a few hangers-on [**doc. 30**].

'The Peelite Party', proclaimed *The Times*, 'is no more' (**102**). Herbert, Graham and Aberdeen agreed. Indeed, the ex-Prime Minister, now more or less in retirement, saw 'the amalgamation of Peel's friends with the liberal party to have practically taken place' (**92**). Only the enigmatic Gladstone refused as yet to accept this publicly, and he was soon given one last chance to prove his Conservative credentials. As the result of a snap vote in the House of Commons on the 'Conspiracy to Murder' Bill, Palmerston was defeated and Derby formed another minority government. Again, as in 1851, he offered Gladstone a place in the Cabinet, this time with greater hope since it was now agreed that Protection was 'not only dead but damned'. Once more Gladstone refused. As he told Derby, he was loath to desert his political friends to join a minority administration; nor did he believe that he would be welcomed by a large section of the Conservative Party. With typical perversity, however, he indicated to the Prime Minister that he was prepared to give general support to the Conservative government, mainly to keep out his immediate *bête noir*, Lord Palmerston. Nevertheless, his refusal to join Derby's Cabinet in 1858 was decisive. It marked for Gladstone the final parting of the ways − intellectually and soon politically − with the Conservative party. He now accepted the truth of Aberdeen's profound remark: 'in this age of progress the liberal party must ultimately govern the country' (**92**). He believed that he had 'great things to do', and that was only possible through membership of a powerful and purposeful government, something which the Conservative Party was unable to provide [**doc. 31**].

Everything now depended on whether the opposition groups in the Commons could combine together to oust the Conservatives and create a new united ministry. 'I see no prospect of the formation of an efficient party', wrote Sidney Herbert at the time, 'let alone Government, out of the chaos on the Opposition benches. No one reigns over or in it, but discord and antipathy' (**93**, ii). Herbert's pessimism was put to the test when at last as a result of the hostility aroused in every section of the Opposition — Whig, Peelite and Radical — by the introduction of the government's reactionary Reform Bill, and its equivocal attitude towards the Italian War of Liberation, they combined together to defeat the Conservatives on 31 March 1859, by 330 votes to 291. In the subsequent general election, though the Conservatives gained about a score of seats, they were still in a minority. It now remained to be seen whether the liberal forces could overcome their differences and join together to form a strong and stable government.

After much patient negotiation by go-betweens, Palmerston and Russell were at last reconciled; and even Gladstone's tender conscience, though it did not allow him to welcome, did not force him to condemn the experiment. The outcome of this moment of truth was the famous meeting at Willis's Rooms on 6 June 1859, when the Whigs, Peelites and Radicals, drawn together primarily by a common sympathy with Italy, agreed to combine together to expel the Conservative government of Derby and Disraeli and establish a new ministry of their own. As a result a government was formed under Lord Palmerston which contained both Lord John Russell (at the Foreign Office) and the leading younger. Peelites, notably Gladstone at the Exchequer, as well as one nominal Radical. It was the establishment of this government that marked the return to an effective two-party system, and ensured eventually the rise of the Gladstonian Liberal Party [**doc. 31**].

Part Three: Assessment

After the collapse of the Tory Party as a result of the reform crisis of 1830–32, it was Sir Robert Peel who emerged as the leader of a new Conservative Party, a position he occupied until the disruption of 1846. The problems he faced were formidable. The Conservatives had been reduced to a rump of 150 MPs after the 1832 general election; the party was divided and demoralised; and, after a long period in which they had been the natural party of government, they were now faced with the arduous and unpalatable task of becoming an effective Opposition. Peel tackled these problems with considerable success. As a result of his strong and effective leadership, his elaboration of Conservative doctrine, the shrewd tactics he deployed in Parliament, and the skills he displayed as Prime Minister in 1834–35, Peel was able to make the Conservative Party a more united and coherent body by the end of the decade, and raise his own status and authority in the Commons and the country. For these reasons, Gash sees Peel as 'the founder of modern Conservatism' (**115**).

As in his Tory days, Peel's fundamental policy remained 'the maintenance of our settled institutions in Church and State'; though this was now perceived in terms of the post-reform *status quo*. This meant opposition to any further organic change in the political system and the defence of the rights of the Church of England; and both implied support for strong government, even if it came under the auspices of the Whigs. Such an attitude was absolutely imperative, Peel believed, at a time when Radicalism, Dissent and the Irish Party were increasingly aggressive and influential. Nevertheless, this Conservative stance did not rule out support for moderate reform: 'the correction of proved abuses and redress of real grievances', in the famous words of the Tamworth Manifesto. This progressive policy was the more necessary if the Conservative Party was to widen the basis of its support and win over the new middle-class voters in the urban areas – 'to conciliate the goodwill of the sober-minded and well-disposed portion of the community'. Peel aimed, therefore, at building up Conservative sentiment in

Parliament and the country, relying on the 'sense, firmness, and moderation' of the Opposition and the deficiencies of the Whigs, and in this he was helped by the efficient management of F. R. Bonham, the party agent, the new Conservative Electoral Committee, and the local party associations.

Peel's strategy appeared to be justified by the overall improvement in the Conservatives' electoral position. In 1835 the Conservatives doubled their numbers in the House of Commons; in 1837 they won 313 seats; in 1841 they obtained 373 seats with an overall majority of eighty, and Peel obtained real power for the first time. For Gash, in his many writings on the period, the great victory of 1841 — in which 'middle-class brains and middle-class votes were essential ingredients' — is the confirmation of Peel's overwhelming success as party leader (**115**). This view, however, has been qualified by other historians. Newbould, in an important article (briefly discussed by Gash in the Foreword to **81**) argues that Peel's attempt to win over the new middle classes to the Conservative Party was largely a failure. In 1841 Conservative electoral strength still lay in the counties and small boroughs in England and Wales; they made practically no headway in the great urban areas or in the 'Celtic Fringe' (**122**). This links up with an even more important point. Gash calls the Conservative Party of this period primarily 'a constitutional and religious party' (**45**). But this appears to underrate seriously the economic basis – the sheer self-interest – of the Conservative Party. As Stewart observes percipiently: 'To look at the Conservative Party through Peel's eyes is distorting; Peel was always more interested in what he thought the party ought to be than in what it was' (**128**). The Conservatives were certainly the party of the Church of England, defiantly and dogmatically; but even more were they the party of the land, the defenders of the Corn Laws and the interests of farmers and landowners. This comes out (as we saw earlier) in their grass-roots propaganda in the general election of 1837 and even more emphatically in 1841; even though of course Peel's personal contribution to the latter victory is undoubted (**51**). 'What triumphed in those elections', writes Newbould, 'were not the Conservative principles of Tamworth, but those aspects of Toryism which Tamworth sought to subvert' (**122**). And this itself shows that Peelite Conservatism had not yet captured the hearts and minds of a majority of the parliamentary party.

These points are just as valid for the 1840s, when in any case constitutional and religious issues were largely pushed into the background. What Peel was trying to do during his second ministry

13916505

was to make the Conservative Party adapt to the needs of a new industrial age; and, in particular, to accept the legitimate claims of the manufacturers to freedom of trade and enterprise. In this he was following in the footsteps of Lord Liverpool (**84**). The interests of 'the field of corn' and 'the field of coal', Peel believed, were complementary rather than in opposition, and both must be subordinated — within the limits of established economic doctrine — to the interests of the nation as a whole. From a party point of view this is the context within which one must see Peel's financial and commercial policies. But to reshape the outlook of the Conservative Party in this way was a difficult, perhaps impossible, task, owing to the extraordinary power of the traditional links between the party and the land. It was, insisted the Tory publicist, J. W. Croker, 'the existence of a landed gentry which has made England what she has been and is' (**7**, iii); and upon the ascendancy of that class depended the maintenance of the established constitution in church and state. However much he might protest to the contrary, the long-term effect of Peel's policies must be to destroy the rightful dominance of the landed interest. Such instinctual responses to the problems of the age — typical of many Tories — were almost immune to rational argument.

Hence, as Peel saw with bitterness, the Conservative Party was prepared to accept with nonchalance many of the outstanding achievements of his ministry after 1841: the containment of the Chartists and O'Connell; financial legislation; social reform; increased prosperity. What moved the backbenchers above all were subjects where their own interests and those of their constituents were concerned; and (as we saw in detail earlier) 'the Agricultural Fanaticks' were becoming more importunate in their demands in the 1840s. This helps to explain the anti-government votes over Canadian corn in 1843, the sugar duties and (indirectly) factory reform in 1844, and Maynooth in the following year. Each successive blow was a clearer warning to Peel that he was rapidly losing touch with the sentiments of many of his followers. The culmination of this process of mutual repulsion was of course the split over the Corn Laws in 1846.

What made this almost inevitable was, on the one hand, the increased pressure on the Commons from the rural constituencies in favour of the Corn Laws, and the emergence of Bentinck as a man who was prepared to use that power to defy the Prime Minister. On the other hand there was Peel's determination to force through repeal come what may. Over this he was as passionate and dogmatic

659

as his opponents – an aspect of Peel which has perhaps been underestimated (**118**). From a long-term point of view what Peel clearly failed to do was to 'educate his party' – to convince them rationally of the merits of repeal. It is doubtful, however, whether this was really possible. There were many reasons for this: Peel's character and temperament, and his growing impatience with and aloofness from his followers in the Commons – an attitude which was largely shared by his closest colleagues, especially Graham (**112**). But it was also due quite simply to the range, complexity and concentration of problems which faced the government and the party in the years between 1842 and 1846. As Gash suggests: 'Peel drove his party in the 1840s too fast and too far' (**115**); but in a sense he had little choice. There was also the implicit but important difference of viewpoint over the significance of 'party' in politics. Peel believed that the purpose of a parliamentary party was to act as the instrument of ministerial decisions; for Bentinck, Disraeli and others, the party's function was to safeguard established principles and act as a source of government policy. But Peel refused to be tied down by what he termed an 'odious servitude' [**doc. 24a**].

In the end the differences between Peel and the bulk of the Conservative Party were irreconcilable. As Greville noted perceptively at the time of his death in July 1850: 'The misfortune of Peel all along was that there was no real community of sentiment between him and his party ... They considered Peel to be not only the minister, but the creature, of the Conservative Party, bound above all things to support and protect their especial interests according to their own views and opinions. He considered himself the Minister of the Nation ...' (**12**, vi).

The year 1846 thus marks the disintegration of the party which Peel had built up so painfully during the decade following the Great Reform Bill. Though there were tentative attempts and hopes of Conservative reunion later, the schism in the end proved permanent. Nevertheless, the influence of Peelite Conservatism continued long after that disruption and the death of the statesman in 1850. The most obvious example of this is the existence of the Peelite group in the House of Commons, small in numbers but large in talent, who occupied a sort of political limbo between the liberals on the one hand and the Protectionists on the other. Yet inexorably the Peelites moved towards the former group. Peel's tenderness towards the Whigs between 1846 and 1850, and the intransigence of the Protectionists over the issue of free trade, helped to stimulate this process. The experience of the Whig-Peelite coalition government of 1852–55 made their ultimate union almost inevitable.

After 1855 there seemed no real alternative to the emergence of a liberal government, given the pressing need for a strong permanent administration that could command the confidence of the Commons and the country. Even Gladstone, the outstanding younger Peelite, despite the emotional tug of his deep-rooted Conservatism, came to accept the logic of events. Besides, as he confided in his diary, he had 'great things to do' and was tired of being out of office (**9**, v). In 1859 he took the plunge and joined Palmerston's government, which brought together all the liberal forces – Whigs, Peelites and Radicals. It was through Gladstone in particular that Peelite ideas were transfused into the new administration. As Chancellor of the Exchequer he became 'the codifier, legislator and guardian of the canons of Peelite finance' (**9**, vii, intro.). Even more was this the case after Gladstone himself became Prime Minister in 1868. In economic matters his outlook remained essentially Peelite during his first ministry and later. As he recorded in the early 1880s: 'I was trained in a Conservative school . . . of Economy, Peace, Sound and strict finance . . . Maintenance of the sound traditions of Parliament and of administration' (**4**, iv). Despite all his earlier criticisms of his old chief, it was Peel who remained Gladstone's master.

Even the Protectionists were in the end influenced by the ideas of the man they had so bitterly attacked. In that sense the trauma of 1846 represented 'a profound process of political education' (**115**). Lord Derby, the Conservative leader, by the time of his second ministry in 1858 was prepared to pay lip service to the doctrine of 'progress'; and in 1867 he became an overnight convert to the principle of 'household suffrage', the basis of the Conservative Reform Act of that year. Disraeli's move away from Protectionist dogma was even more precipitate and emphatic. As early as 1852 he announced that Protection was 'not only dead but damned'. After 1868, in his attempt as Conservative leader to cultivate the urban middle classes, to emphasise the common interests of industrial and landed property, and to identify his party with a doctrine of necessary reform, Disraeli was pursuing 'a line of policy closely comparable to the outlook and approach of Peel' (**125**). But Disraeli, characteristically, also gave the Conservative Party something more: the mythology of 'Tory Democracy'. For Professor Gash, however, commenting in 1961 on the party's modern history, 'though the myth of Conservatism has been more often Disraelian, its practice has been almost uniformly Peelite' (**80**). In the age of Margaret Thatcher, it may be suggested, both labels have been rendered obsolete.

Part Four: Documents

The Tory Government and Peterloo

This extract shows the government's deliberate support for the local magistrates after Peterloo (1819), and opposition to popular protest. The 'strong measures' referred to were passed the same year as the notorious Six Acts.

You will naturally ask whether the proceedings of the magistrates at Manchester on the 16th were really justifiable. To this I answer, in the first instance, that all the papers on which they proceeded were laid before the Chancellor, and the Attorney and Solicitor-General, and that they were fully satisfied that the meeting was of a character and description, and assembled under such circumstances, as justified the magistrates in dispersing it by force.

When I say that the proceedings of the magistrates at Manchester on the 16th ult. were justifiable, you will understand me as not by any means deciding that the course which they pursued on that occasion was in all its parts prudent. A great deal might be said in their favour even on this head; but, whatever judgment might be formed in this respect, being satisfied that they were substantially right, there remained no alternative but to support them; and I am sorry to say that, notwithstanding the support which they have received, there prevails such a panic throughout that part of the country that it is difficult to get either magistrates to act or witnesses to come forward to give evidence, and that many of the lower orders who were supposed loyal have joined the disaffected, partly from fear, and partly from a conviction that some great change was near at hand . . .

When Parliament does meet, it will be indispensably necessary to consider what measures can be adopted for averting those evils with which the country is so seriously threatened by the frequency of these seditious meetings, and still more perhaps by the outrageous licentiousness of the Press.

The remedies are undoubtedly full of difficulty. The question must be, is the country ripe for strong and effectual measures on these points; and, how long can we venture to wait, and go on without them?

Lord Liverpool to Canning, 23 September 1819, quoted in **96**, ii, pp. 410—11.

document 2

The Tories and parliamentary reform

Lord Liverpool's comments on parliamentary reform were sparked off by the proposed disfranchisement of the notoriously corrupt borough of Grampound in 1821. In accordance with his sentiments the seat was in fact given to the county of Yorkshire.

Memorandum by Lord Liverpool
I cannot agree in opinion with the writer of the enclosed memorandum. I assume what remains to be proved, that the boro' of Grampound is so corrupt as to require to be disfranchised . . . I should then say that the giving the right of election to the populous manufacturing towns was the worst remedy which could be applied. In the first place, it would be the greatest evil conferred on those towns; it would subject the population to a perpetual factious canvass, which would divert, more or less, the people from their industrious habits, and keep alive a permanent spirit of turbulence and disaffection among them.

Against such a measure all the most respectable inhabitants of those towns would, I was convinced, protest . . . In the next place, I think the proposed transfer would be the most injurious to the Constitution that could be devised.

I do not wish to see more such boroughs as Westminster, Southwark, Nottingham, etc. I believe them to be more corrupt than any other places when seriously contested; and I believe the description of persons which find their way into Parliament through these places are generally those who, from the peculiarity of their character or their station, are the least likely to be steadily attached to the good order of society . . . I should prefer transferring the members to the larger counties. County elections are the least corrupt of any in the kingdom. The representatives of them, if not severally the ablest members in the House, are certainly those who have the greatest stake in the country, and may be trusted for the most part in periods of difficulty and danger.

From **96**, iii, pp. 137–8.

Peel and Canning

In this letter Peel explains why he refused to serve under Canning as Prime Minister after the retirement of Lord Liverpool. Despite his reputation as a liberal Tory, it reveals his strong anti-Catholic position at this time.

The letter which I have received from you gives me the opportunity of recording, and indeed makes it necessary that I should record, the grounds on which I felt myself compelled to decline being a member of the Administration over which you are to preside as Prime Minister.

I do not consider that my objections to remain in office resolve themselves merely into a point of honour. The grounds on which I decline office are public grounds, clear and intelligible, I think, to every man who has marked the course which I have pursued in Parliament on the Catholic question, and who understands the nature and the functions of the office which I have filled.

For the period of eleven years I have been connected with the Administration over which Lord Liverpool presided. During the whole of that period, indeed during the whole of my public career, I have taken a very active and prominent part in opposition to the Catholic claims, concurring in opinion and acting in unison with the head of the Government of which I was a member.

Can I see the whole influence and authority of the office of Prime Minister transferred from Lord Liverpool to you without a conviction that the sanguine hopes of the Roman Catholics will be excited, and that the Catholic question will be practically and materially affected by the change?

It is not merely that you differ from Lord Liverpool on the Catholic question. It is the extent of the difference which must be regarded. It is that the opinions avowed by Lord Liverpool on the last occasion on which he had an opportunity of avowing them must be compared with those opinions which you have uniformly and so powerfully enforced. The transfer of the influence of Prime Minister from Lord Liverpool to you is the transfer of that influence from the most powerful opponent to the most powerful advocate of the Roman Catholic claims.

If I were to be a party to the arrangement by accepting office under it, I should (always bearing in mind the particular situation in which I am placed) be subject to great misconstruction, and, in fact, should be lending myself to the advancement of a cause which under a different aspect of political affairs I had uniformly and strenuously resisted . . .

Such are the grounds on which, most reluctantly, but without hesitation, I felt myself compelled to relinquish office.

Peel to Canning, 17 April 1827, quoted in **10**, i, pp. 466—8.

document 4
The fall of Wellington's government, 1830

Mrs Arbuthnot was the wife of the government Whip, Charles Arbuthnot, an Ultra Tory and confidante of the Duke of Wellington.

Nov. 10th. — The Guildhall dinner was given up in consequence of the threatening aspect of the mob, and the Lord Mayor coming to Sir Robt Peel to say that he c^d not answer for the maintenance of the peace of the City. The pickpockets & thieves of London are so exasperated against the new Police that they had determined to have a *row*. It is supposed they intended to disable the horses in the carriages and then attack the persons inside and take their chance of plunder and murder. The Duke of Wellington is their great object of hatred just now.

15th. — London is perfectly tranquil again and there has been no more mobbing, but every day only proves more & more how impossible it is to go on with the Cabinet constituted as it now is in the H. of Commons.

20th. — At length we have broke down! On Monday last, the 15th, on the debate whether the Civil List sh^d be referred to a Committee or not, a question of no sort of consequence, the ultra-Tories united with the Whigs & Hume, & we were beat by 29.

I was dining at the Duke of Wellington's with the Prince of Orange and a large party when the Duke got a note telling him what had happened, & that Peel, Goulburn & Mr Arbuthnot were come up to talk to him. He whispered to me before he went down what had happened, & went away, saying nothing to anyone else. I stayed till they were all gone & then went down stairs and heard *all about it*. I never saw a man so delighted as Peel. He said, when the Opposition cheered at the division that he did not join in it but that it was with difficulty he refrained, he was so delighted at having so good an opportunity for resigning.

It was agreed the Duke sh^d go the next morning to the King and tell him that, having had this proof of the want of confidence of the H. of Commons in the Gov^t, they must resign. He accordingly did this. The King was excessively distressed, asked him whether it was really inevitable, whether no junction c^d be formed, no strength gained, said that he had unbounded confidence in the Duke & that, if there was anything he c^d do to prevent this misfortune, he was willing to do it & w^d stand by him to the last. He cried & was in the greatest possible agitation. The Duke told him it was impossible; that, for his (the King's) own sake, he had better try another arrangement. He expressed unbounded gratitude for the King's kindness & the deepest regret at being unable to continue to serve him. The King saw Peel and, finding the resignation must be accepted, he acquiesced & sent for Lord Grey.

From *The Journal of Mrs. Arbuthnot*, November 1830, **2**, ii, pp. 400—02.

document 5

'Tory' or 'Conservative'

After 1830 the term 'Conservative' began to displace the traditional term 'Tory' to describe the Opposition. It was first used in its contemporary sense in the following extract from an article written by an anonymous journalist.

If it should be inferred, from any of the observations which have now been made, that any alteration has taken place in our political views or principles, we beg to repel the accusation. Should it be expected of us, we have no reluctance distinctly to avow our political opinions. We despise and abominate the details of partisan warfare, but we now are, as we always have been, decidedly and conscientiously attached to what is called the Tory, and which might with more propriety be called the Conservative, party; a party which we believe to compose by far the largest, wealthiest, and most intelligent and respectable portion of the population of this country, and without whose support any administration that can be formed will be found deficient both in character and stability. Some of this party, we know, object to all change whatever; and, by the obstinacy they have displayed on this point, and the coldness and distance which have too often marked their demeanour, they have, in our judgement, done essential injury to the side to which they belong. But these are neither considerable in numbers, in rank, or in influence. We have no hesitation in stating it to be our conviction, that an immense majority of the *tories* are as anxious to promote any prudent and practicable amelioration of the state, as any of their fellow-subjects; and we must take leave to say that we cannot conceive on what grounds their political opponents have supposed themselves to be entitled to the exclusive privilege of entertaining or uttering patriotic or independent sentiments.

From the *Quarterly Review*, January 1830.

document 6

Disraeli on Peel

Despite the author's hostility to Peel during the 1840s, this extract shows Disraeli's sympathy and perception.

Nature had combined in Sir Robert Peel many admirable parts. In him a physical frame incapable of fatigue was united with an understanding equally vigorous and flexible. He was gifted with the faculty of method in the highest degree; and with great powers of application which were sustained by a prodigious memory; while he could communicate his acquisitions with clear and fluent elocution.

Such a man, under any circumstances and in any sphere of life, would probably have become remarkable. Ordained from his youth to be busied with the affairs of a great empire, such a man, after long years of observation, practice, and perpetual discipline would have become what Sir Robert Peel was in the latter portion of his life, a transcendent administrator of public business and a matchless master of debate in a popular assembly.

Thus gifted and thus accomplished, Sir Robert Peel had a great deficiency; he was without imagination. Wanting imagination, he wanted prescience. No one was more sagacious when dealing with the circumstances before him; no one penetrated the present with more acuteness and accuracy. His judgment was faultless provided he had not to deal with the future. Thus it happened through his long career, that while he always was looked upon as the most prudent and safest of leaders, he ever, after a protracted display of admirable tactics, concluded his campaigns by surrendering at discretion. He was so adroit that he could prolong resistance even beyond its term, but so little foreseeing that often in the very triumph of his manoeuvres he found himself in an untenable position. And so it came to pass that Roman Catholic emancipation, parliamentary reform, and the abrogation of our commercial system, were all carried in haste or in passion and without conditions or mitigatory arrangements.

Sir Robert Peel had a peculiarity which is perhaps natural with men of very great talents who have not the creative faculty; he had a dangerous sympathy with the creations of others. Instead of being cold and wary, as was commonly supposed, he was impulsive and even inclined to rashness . . .

Sir Robert Peel had a bad manner of which he was sensible; he was by nature very shy, but forced early in life into eminent positions, he had formed an artificial manner, haughtily stiff or exuberantly bland, of which, generally speaking, he could not divest himself. There were, however, occasions when he did succeed in this, and on these, usually when he was alone with an individual whom he wished to please, his manner was not only unaffectedly cordial, but he could even charm. . . .

For so very clever a man he was deficient in the knowledge of human nature. The prosperous routine of his youth was not favourable to the development of this faculty. It was never his lot to struggle; although forty years in Parliament, it is remarkable that Sir Robert Peel never represented a popular constituency or stood a contested election.

From Benjamin Disraeli, *Lord George Bentinck*, (1852), Constable 1905 ed., pp. 198–203.

document 7
Peel and parliamentary reform

Here Peel explains his reasons for opposing the Whig Reform Bill of 1831.

But, Sir, if this feeling be such as we have heard it represented, and if it shall permanently endure, I am then ready to admit, that no government can go on without enacting such measures as shall alleviate and remove that intense feeling. But all I ask is, time for deliberation upon a question of such vital importance; I say, do not rely upon this temporary excitement – do not allow that to be your only guide – do not force this Reform Bill upon the country, upon the assumption that the unanimous voice of the people demands it.

I doubt the existence of any such ground; and if you do find hereafter that you have been mistaken — if you find that the people have only been acting under an excitement produced by temporary causes — if they are already sobering down from their enthusiasm for the days of July, let the House remember, that when the steady good sense and reason of the people of England shall return, they will be the first to reproach us with the baseness of having sacrificed the constitution in the vain hope of conciliating the favour of a temporary burst of popular feeling; they will be the first to blame us for deferring this question to popular opinion, instead of acting upon our own judgment. For my own part, not seeing the necessity for this reform, doubting much whether the demand for reform is so urgent, and doubting still more whether, if carried, this measure can be a permanent one, I give my conscientious opposition to this bill. In doing this, I feel the more confident, because the bill does not fulfil the conditions recommended from the throne — because it is not founded on the acknowledged principles of the constitution — because it does not give security to the prerogatives of the Crown — because it does not guarantee the legitimate rights, influences, and privileges of both Houses of Parliament — because it is not calculated to render secure and permanent the happiness and prosperity of the people — and above all, because it subverts a system of government which has combined security to personal liberty, and protection to property, with vigour in the executive power of the State, in a more perfect degree than ever existed in any age, or in any other country of the world.

Speech in the House of Commons, 6 July 1831, quoted in **11**, ii, pp. 333.

document 8
Peel in Opposition

In this letter to a colleague Peel indicates the tactics he believed should be pursued by the Opposition in order to restore Conservative support in the country.

I presume the chief object of that party which is called Conservative, whatever its number may be, will be to resist Radicalism, to prevent those further encroachments of democratic influence which will be attempted (probably successfully attempted) as the natural consequence of the triumph already achieved.

I certainly think that − as that party will be comparatively weak in numbers; as victories gained by mere union with the Radicals will promote mainly the views of the Radicals; as there is no use in defeating, no use in excluding a Government, unless you can replace it by one formed on principles more consonant to your own − our policy ought to be rather to conciliate the goodwill of the sober-minded and well-disposed portion of the community, and thus lay the foundation of future strength, than to urge an opposition on mere party grounds, and for the purpose of mere temporary triumph.

I think it is very difficult to lay down any course of action in detail. Circumstances which we cannot foresee or control will determine that. I should recommend a system of caution and observation at the first commencement of the Session, rather than that we should be the first to take the field, or instantly begin hostilities. We act on the defensive. The Radicals must move, they must attack. We can, in my opinion, act with more effect after that attack shall have commenced than before.

The best position the Government could assume would be that of moderation between opposite extremes of Ultra-Toryism and Radicalism. We should appear to the greatest advantage in defending the Government, whenever the Government espoused our principles, as I apprehend they must do if they mean to maintain the cause of authority and order.

Possibly we shall find them indifferent to this, and afraid of an open rupture with the Radicals. In that case we must oppose their united forces with all the energy we can, but even so our power will be greater should the union which we resist appear to be the voluntary deliberate act of the Government, rather than an act forced upon them by our precipitate or unreasonable opposition.

Peel to Goulburn, 3 January 1833, quoted in **10**, ii, pp. 212−13.

document 9

Peel and the Great Reform Bill

In this famous speech Peel accepts the Reform Bill as a fait accompli, *and determines to 'look forward to the future alone'.*

The king's government had abstained from all unseemly triumph in the king's speech respecting the measure of reform. He would profit by their example, and would say nothing upon that head; but consider that question as finally and irrevocably disposed of. He was now determined to look forward to the future alone, and considering the constitution as it existed, to take his stand on main and essential matters — to join in resisting every attempt at new measures, which could not be stirred without unsettling the public mind, and endangering public prosperity. It should be widely known that the industrious classes could only subsist by public tranquillity — by the existence of those habits of obedience, and that general order which would allow men possessed of property to bring their capital into operation; and that the welfare of the labouring — he would not say lower — classes was secured by the peaceful enjoyment of all property, and by avoiding those measures which must increase the apprehensions he was confident existed in the minds of capitalists. There were, he was aware, no means of governing this country but through the House of Commons: and therefore he, humble as he was, was determined to take his stand in defence of law and order — in defence of the King's throne, and the security of the empire — from motives as truly independent as those by which any member of the most liberal opinions, and representing the largest constituency in the kingdom, was actuated.

Speech in the House of Commons, 7 February 1833, quoted in **11**, ii, pp. 612–13.

document 10

Peel in 1834

Greville's account well illustrates Peel's increased power and authority in the House of Commons at this time, though he was not yet accepted as official party leader. Charles Greville was Clerk to the Privy Council, and Whiggish in sympathy.

Went to the H. of Commons last night, where I have not been for many years. A great change, a thorough set of blackguards, and hardly a human being whose face I knew ...

Peel spoke very shortly, but very well indeed. Peel's is an enviable position; in the prime of life, with an immense fortune, *facile Princeps* in the House of Commons, unshackled by Party connexions and prejudices, universally regarded as the ablest man, and with (on the whole) a very high character, free from the cares of office, able to devote himself to literature, to politics, or idleness, as the fancy takes him. No matter how unruly the House, how impatient or fatigued, the moment he rises all is silence, and he is sure of being heard with profound attention and respect. This is the enjoyable period of his life, and he must make the most of it, for when time and the hour shall bring about his return to power, his cares and anxieties will begin, and with whatever success his ambition may hereafter be crowned, he will hardly fail to look back with regret to this holyday time of his political career. How free and light he must feel at being liberated from the shackles of his old connexions, and at being able to take any part that his sense of his own interests or of the public exigencies may point out! And then the satisfactory consciousness of being by far the most eminent man in the House of Commons, to see and feel the respect He inspires and the consideration He enjoys. . .

His great merit consists in his judgement, tact, and discretion, his facility, promptitude, thorough knowledge of the assembly he addresses, familiarity with the details of every sort of Parliamentary business, and the great command he has over himself. He never was a great favourite of mine, but I am satisfied that he is the fittest man to be Minister, and I therefore wish to see him return to power.

From *The Greville Memoirs*, 22 February 1834, **12**, iii, pp. 18—19.

document 11

The Tamworth Manifesto

The extract below, the key section of the Manifesto delivered by Peel to his parliamentary constituency on the eve of the general election of 1835, expressed the central ideas of Peelite Conservatism.

Now I say at once that I will not accept power on the condition of declaring myself an apostate from the principles on which I have heretofore acted. At the same time, I never will admit that I have been, either before or after the Reform Bill, the defender of abuses, or the enemy of judicious reforms. . . . I have not been disposed to acquiesce in acknowledged evils, either from the mere superstitious reverence for ancient usages, or from the dread of labour or responsibility in the application of a remedy . . .

With respect to the Reform Bill itself, I will repeat now the declaration which I made when I entered the House of Commons as a Member of the Reformed Parliament, that I consider the Reform Bill a final and irrevocable settlement of a great Constitutional question — a settlement which no friend to the peace and welfare of this country would attempt to disturb, either by direct or by insidious means.

Then, as to the spirit of the Reform Bill, and the willingness to adopt and enforce it as a rule of government: if, by adopting the spirit of the Reform Bill, it be meant that we are to live in a perpetual vortex of agitation; that public men can only support themselves in public estimation by adopting every popular impression of the day, — by promising the instant redress of anything which anybody may call an abuse, — by abandoning altogether that great aid of government — more powerful than either law or reason — the respect for ancient rights, and the deference to prescriptive authority; if this be the spirit of the Reform Bill, I will not undertake to adopt it. But if the spirit of the Reform Bill implies merely a careful review of institutions, civil and ecclesiastical, undertaken in a friendly temper, combining, with the firm maintenance of established rights, the correction of proved abuses and the redress of real grievances, — in that case, I can for myself and colleagues undertake to act in such a spirit and with such intentions.

Quoted in **6**, pp. 76−7.

document 12

The general election of 1841

Greville here provides a perceptive summary of the reasons for the Conservative victory in the general election.

The elections are sufficiently over to exhibit a pretty certain result, and the termination of the great Yorkshire contest by the signal victory of the Tories — a defeat, the magnitude of which there is no possibility of palliating, or finding any excuse for — seems to have had the effect of closing the contest. The Whigs give the whole thing up as irretrievably lost; and though some of them with whom I have conversed still maintain that they did right to dissolve, they do not affect to deny that the result has disappointed all their hopes and calculations, and been disastrous beyond their worst fears; and they now give Peel a majority of sixty or seventy. The most remarkable thing has been the erroneous calculations on both sides as to particular places, each having repeatedly lost when they thought the gain most certain. The Whigs complain bitterly of the apathy and indifference that have prevailed, and cannot recover from their surprise that their promises of cheap bread and cheap sugar have not proved more attractive. But they do not comprehend the real cause of this apathy. It is true that there has not been any violent Tory reaction, because there have been no great topics on which enthusiasm could fasten, but there has been a revival of Conservative influence, which has been gradually increasing for some time, and together with it a continually decreasing confidence in the Government. They have been getting more unpopular every day with almost all classes, and when they brought forward their Budget the majority of the country, even those who approved of its principles, gave them little or no credit for the measure, and besides doubting whether the advantages it held out were very great or important, believed that their real motives and object were to recover the popularity they had lost, and to make a desperate plunge to maintain themselves in office. It was all along my opinion that their dissolution was a great blunder, that they would have consulted their own party interests better, and still more certainly the success of the fiscal measures they advocate, by resigning after their vote of confidence. But they thought they could get up excitement, and by agitation place matters in such a state that their successors would be unable to govern the country.

From *The Greville Memoirs*, 11 July 1841, **12**, iv, pp. 392–3.

document 13
The duties of a Prime Minister

Peel's letter vividly illustrates his tasks as a Prime Minister — and why he was so often out of touch with his backbenchers.

I defy the Minister of this country to perform properly the duties of his office — to read all that he ought to read, including the whole foreign correspondence; to keep up the constant communication with the Queen, *and the Prince*; to see all whom he ought to see; to superintend the grant of honours and the disposal of civil and ecclesiastical patronage; to write with his own hand to every person of note who chooses to write to him; to be prepared for every debate, including the most trumpery concerns; to do all these indispensable things, and also sit in the House of Commons eight hours a day for 118 days.

It is impossible for me not to feel that the duties are incompatible, and above all human strength — at least above mine.

The worst of it is that the really important duties to the country — those out of the House of Commons — are apt to be neglected.

Peel to Arbuthnot, 14 August 1845, quoted in **10**, iii, pp. 218–19.

document 14

The Plug Riots, 1842

The letter from Sir James Graham, the Home Secretary, describes the disorders in the North at this time, and illustrates, implicitly, his own views on their causes and character.

Sir James Graham with humble duty begs to lay before your Majesty the general result of the information which has reached him to-day from the disturbed districts.

At Preston the good effect of vigorous measures has been demonstrated by the return of the workpeople to their employment.

At Blackburn Colonel Arbuthnot resisted the entrance of the mob into the town with success. No lives were lost, and the ringleaders were apprehended.

At Manchester peace was preserved, but all labour was suspended. A great concourse from the surrounding district was expected to assemble to-day. The railway communications had been threatened.

Huddersfield has been attacked by a mob, and Wakefield threatened.

Sir James Graham has called on the Duke of Rutland to repair to his county, and to assemble the Yeomanry in Leicestershire, where among the colliers the same organised disposition unhappily has shown itself, to cease from working and compel by force cessation of labour.

In Warwickshire also some disturbances have occurred, and in the Pottery district houses have been burnt and plundered in open day.

In some of the disturbed counties Sir James Graham was by no means satisfied with the activity of the magistrates; and the mill-owners have shown a want of proper spirit in defending their property. He, in consequence, addressed a circular to the Lords Lieutenant . . .

At Manchester a body of delegates is assembled, which evidently directs the whole operation as from a common centre. Sir James Graham has ordered these delegates to be apprehended.

Graham to Queen Victoria, 16 August 1842, quoted in **90**, i, pp. 320–1.

document 15

Peel's Budget, 1842

Greville's praise is typical of many contemporary estimates.

On Friday night in the midst of the most intense and general interest and curiosity, heightened by the closeness and fidelity with which the Government measures had been kept secret Peel brought forward his financial plans in a speech of three hours and forty minutes, acknowledged by everybody to have been a masterpiece of financial statement. The success was complete; he took the House by storm; and his Opponents (though of course differing and objecting on particular points) did him ample justice. A few people expected an income tax, but the majority did not. Hitherto the Opposition have been talking very big about opposing all taxes, but they have quite altered their tone. It is really remarkable to see the attitude Peel has taken in this Parliament, his complete mastery over both his friends and his foes. His own party, *nolentes aut volentes*, have surrendered at discretion, and he has got them as well disciplined and as obedient as the crew of a man-of-war. This great measure, so lofty in conception, right in direction, and able in execution, places him at once on a pinnacle of power, and establishes his Government on such a foundation as accident alone can shake. Political predictions are always rash, but certainly there is every probability of Peel's being Minister for as many years as his health and vigour may endure . . . There can be no doubt that he is now a very great man, and it depends on himself to establish a great and lasting reputation.

From *The Greville Memoirs*, 13 March 1842, **12**, v, pp. 16–17.

document 16

The Conservatives and social reform

These two extracts from the debates on the Factory Bill of 1844 illustrate the arguments of the supporters of the ten-hour day (Lord Ashley) and of its opponents, here represented by Sir James Graham, speaking for the government.

Lord Ashley: Sir, under all the aspects in which it can be viewed, this system of things must be abrogated or restrained — it affects the internal tranquillity of those vast provinces, and all relations between employer and employed — it forms a perpetual grievance and ever comes uppermost among their complaints in all times of difficulty and discontent. It disturbs the order of nature, and the rights of the labouring men, by ejecting the males from the workshop, and filling their places by females, who are thus withdrawn from all their domestic duties and exposed to insufferable toil at half the wages that would be assigned to males, for the support of their families. It affects — nay, more, it absolutely annihilates, all the arrangements and provisions of domestic economy — thrift and management are altogether impossible; had they twice the amount of their present wages, they would be but slightly benefited — everything runs to waste; the house and children are deserted; the wife can do nothing for her husband and family; she can neither cook, wash, repair clothes, nor take charge of the infants; all must be paid for out of her scanty earnings, and, after all, most imperfectly done. Dirt, discomfort, ignorance, recklessness, are the portion of such households; the wife has no time for learning in her youth, and none for practice in her riper age; the females are most unequal to the duties of the men in the factories; and all things go to rack and ruin, because the men can discharge at home no one of the especial duties that Providence has assigned to the females. Why need I detain the House by a specification of these injurious results? They will find them stated at painful length in the Second Report of the Children's Employment Commission. Consider it, too, under its physical aspect! Will the House turn a deaf ear to the complaints of suffering that resound from all quarters? Will it be indifferent to the physical consequences on the rising generation? . . . But every consideration sinks to nothing compared with that which springs from the contemplation of the moral mischiefs this system engenders and sustains. You are poisoning the very sources of order and happiness and virtue; you are tearing up, root and branch, all the relations of families to each other; you are annulling, as it were, the institution of domestic life, decreed by Providence Himself, the wisest and kindest of earthly ordinances, the mainstay of social peace and virtue, and therein of national security.

Sir James Graham: The noble lord said, the time is come when, in his opinion, it is necessary to lay the axe to the root of the tree. Before we do this let me entreat the Committee carefully to consider what is that tree which we are to lay prostrate. If it be, as I suppose, the tree of the commercial greatness of this country, I am satisfied that although some of its fruits may be bitter, yet upon the whole it has produced that greatness, that wealth, that prosperity, which make these small islands most remarkable in the history of the civilised world, which, upon the whole, diffuse happiness amidst this great community, and render this nation one of the most civilised, if not the most civilised, and powerful on the face of the globe. . .

My noble friend stated that he would not enter into the commercial part of the question; but if I can show that the inevitable result of the abridgement of time will be the diminution of wages to the employed, then I say, with reference to the interests of the working classes themselves, there never was a more doubtful question before Parliament than this. . . . Then in the close race of competition which our manufacturers are now running with foreign competitors, it must be considered what effect this reduction of one-sixth of the hours of labour would have upon them. The question in its bearing upon competition must be carefully considered; and I have been informed that in that respect such a step would be fatal to many of our manufacturers — a feather would turn the scale: an extra pound weight would lose the race. But that would not be the first effect. The first effect would fall upon the operative. It is notorious that a great part of the power of the mill-owners, a power which alone justifies such legislation as this, arises from the redundant supply of labour. It follows that when a master is pressed upon by your legislation, he will compensate himself by forcing upon those in his employ a decrease of wages. I believe the large majority of intelligent operatives comprehend that proposition thoroughly. I have seen many, and conversed with them, and they have admitted that the proposal involves a necessary decrease of wages.

From *Parliamentary Debates, 1844,* quoted in **1**, pp. 599–605.

document 17

Disraeli on Peelite Conservatism

In this famous extract from his novel, Disraeli is attacking Peelite Conservatism through the mouths of Tadpole and Taper – typical party wire-pullers of the period. The reference is to the general election of 1841.

In the meantime, after dinner, Tadpole and Taper, who were among the guests of Mr. Ormsby, withdrew to a distant sofa, out of earshot, and indulged in confidential talk. . . .

'Ah! Tadpole,' said Mr. Taper, getting a little maudlin; 'I often think, if the time should ever come, when you and I should be joint secretaries of the Treasury.'

'We shall see, we shall see. All we have to do is to get into Parliament, work well together, and keep other men down.'

'We will do our best,' said Taper. 'A dissolution you hold inevitable?'

'How are you and I to get into Parliament, if there be not one? We must make it inevitable. I tell you what, Taper, the lists must prove a dissolution inevitable. You understand me? If the present Parliament goes on, where shall we be? We shall have new men cropping up every session.'

'True, terribly true,' said Mr. Taper. 'That we should ever live to see a Tory Government again! We have reason to be very thankful.'

'Hush!' said Mr. Tadpole. "That time has gone by for Tory Governments; what the country requires is a sound Conservative Government.'

'A sound Conservative Government,' said Taper musingly. 'I understand: Tory men and Whig measures.'

From Benjamin Disraeli, *Coningsby*, 1844, ch. VI.

document 18
Disraeli on Maynooth

Disraeli's arguments against the Maynooth grant were poor; but as a personal diatribe against Peel the speech was immensely effective.

If you are to have a popular Government — if you are to have a Parliamentary Administration the conditions antecedent are, that you should have a Government which declares the principles upon which its policy is founded, and then you can have the wholesome check of a constitutional Opposition. What have we got instead? Something has risen up in this country as fatal in the political world, as it has been in the landed world of Ireland — we have a great Parliamentary middleman. It is well known what a middleman is; he is a man who bamboozles one party and plunders the other, till, having obtained a position to which he is not entitled, he cries out, 'Let us have no party questions, but fixity of tenure'. . .

Let us in this House re-echo that which I believe to be the sovereign sentiment of this country; let us tell persons in high places that cunning is not caution, and that habitual perfidy is not high policy of State. On that ground we may all join. Let us bring back to this House that which it has for so long a time past been without — the legitimate influence and salutary check of a constitutional Opposition. Let us do it at once in the only way in which it can be done, by dethroning this dynasty of deception, by putting an end to the intolerable yoke of official despotism and Parliamentary imposture.

From *Parliamentary Debates*, 11 April 1845, quoted in **74**, pp. 188–9.

document 19

Ashley's Ten-hour Bill, 1844

Ashley's ten-hour amendment to the government's Factory Bill was passed on 15 March by 179 votes to 170. Greville describes the circumstances of the defeat.

I never remember so much excitement as has been caused by Ashley's Ten Hours Bill, nor a more curious political state of things, such intermingling of parties, such a confusion of opposition; a question so much more open than any question ever was before, and yet not made so or acknowledged to be so with the Government; so much zeal, asperity, and animosity, so many reproaches hurled backwards and forwards. The Government have brought forward their measure in a very positive way, and have clung to it with great tenacity, rejecting all compromise; they have been abandoned by nearly half their supporters, and nothing can exceed their chagrin and soreness at being so forsaken. Some of them attribute it to Graham's unpopularity, and aver that if Peel had brought it forward, or if a meeting had been previously called, they would not have been defeated; again, some declare that Graham had said they were indifferent to the result, and that people might vote as they pleased, which he stoutly denies . . .

The House did certainly put itself in an odd predicament, with its two votes directly opposed to each other. The whole thing is difficult and unpleasant. Government will carry their Bill now, and Ashley will be able to do nothing, but he will go on agitating session after session; and a Philanthropic agitator is more dangerous than a repealer, either of the Union or the Corn Laws. We are just now over run with philanthropy, and God knows where it will stop, or whither it will lead us.

From *The Greville Memoirs*, 31 March 1844, **12**, v, pp. 169–70.

document 20

The government and the country gentlemen

Like Peel, Graham strongly resented the anti-government votes of the Conservative backbenchers between 1842 and 1845. He argued – rightly as it turned out – that this must ultimately lead to the downfall of the government.

I am aware of the fact that our country gentlemen are out of humour, and that the existence of the Government is endangered by their present temper and recent proceedings. We have laboured hard, and not in vain, to restore the prosperity of the country, not to give increased security to the aristocracy, by improving the condition and diminishing the discontent of the great masses of the people. We have effected this object without inflicting any real injury on the landed proprietors; yet we are scouted as traitors, and are denounced as if we were time-serving traders in politics, seeking to retain place by the sacrifice of the interests of our friends.

The country gentlemen cannot be more ready to give us the death-blow than we are prepared to receive it. If they will rush on their own destruction, they must have their way: we have endeavoured to save them, and they regard us as enemies for so doing.

If we have lost the confidence and good will of the country party, our official days are numbered; and the time will come when this party will bitterly deplore the fall of Sir Robert Peel, and when in vain they will wish that they had not overthrown a Government which its enemies could not vanquish, but which its supporters abandoned and undermined.

Graham to Croker, 22 March 1845, quoted in **7**, ii, p. 31.

document 21

Peel and the Corn Laws crisis

The following two documents illustrate (a) Peel's first response to the Irish famine and his belief that it rendered the Corn Laws out of date; and (b) the background to his decision.

(a)   CABINET MEMORANDUM, November 1.

If we can place confidence in the Reports which we have received, there is the prospect of a lamentable deficiency of the ordinary food of the people in many parts of Ireland, and in some parts of this country, and of Scotland. The evil *may be* much greater than present reports lead us to anticipate . . .

It compels an immediate decision on these questions.

Shall we maintain unaltered —

Shall we modify —

Shall we suspend — the operation of the Corn Laws?

Can we vote public money for the sustenance of any considerable portion of the people on account of actual or apprehended scarcity, and maintain in full operation the existing restrictions on the free import of grain?

I am bound to say my impression is that we cannot . . .

I cannot disguise from myself that the calling together of Parliament on account of apprehended scarcity — the prohibition of export in other countries — the removal of restrictions on import (sanctioned, as in the case of Belgium, by an unanimous vote of the Chambers) — the demand for public money, to be applied to provide sustenance for a portion of the people — will constitute a great crisis, and that it will be dangerous for the Government, having assembled Parliament, to resist with all its energies any material modification of the Corn Law. [There is] . . . the necessity of determining, before we resolve on calling Parliament, the course we shall pursue. We must make our choice between determined maintenance, modification, and suspension of the existing Corn Law.

In writing the above I have merely considered the question on its own abstract merits, without reference to mere party considerations, or our own position as public men, the authors of the present Corn Law. I am fully aware of the gravity of the considerations connected with this part of the question.

ROBERT PEEL.

Cabinet Memorandum. 1 November 1845, quoted in **10**, ii, pp. 141–8.

(b) It is to his *own* talent and firmness that Sir Robert will owe his success, which cannot fail. He said he had been determined not to go to a general election with the fetters the last election had imposed upon him, and he had meant at the end of the next Session to call the whole Conservative Party together and to declare this to them, that he would not meet another Parliament pledged to the maintenance of the Corn Laws, which could be maintained no longer, and that he would make a public declaration to this effect before another general election came on. This had been defeated by events coming too suddenly upon him, and he had no alternative but to deal with the Corn Laws before a national calamity would *force* it on. The League had made immense progress, and had enormous means at their disposal. If he had resigned in November, Lord Stanley and the Protectionists would have been prepared to form a Government, and a Revolution might have been the consequence of it. Now they felt that it was too late.

Sir Robert has *an immense scheme in view*; he thinks he shall be able to remove the contest entirely from the dangerous ground upon which it has got — that of a war between the manufacturers, the hungry and the poor against the landed proprietors, the aristocracy, which can only end in the ruin of the latter; he will not bring forward a measure upon the Corn Laws, but a much more comprehensive one. He will deal with the whole commercial system of the country. He will adopt the principle of the League, *that of removing all protection and abolishing all monopoly*, but not in favour of one class and as a triumph over another, but to the benefit of the nation, farmers as well as manufacturers.

Memorandum by Prince Albert, 25 December 1845, quoted in **6**, pp. 130–1.

document 22

The fall of Sir Robert Peel

Disraeli's famous account describes the vote of the Protectionists on the Irish Coercion Bill, 25 June 1846, which (in alliance with the Whigs) brought down Peel's government.

But it was not merely their numbers that attracted the anxious observation of the treasury bench as the protectionists passed in defile before the minister to the hostile lobby. It was impossible that he could have marked them without emotion: the flower of that great party which had been so proud to follow one who had been so proud to lead them. They were men to gain whose hearts and the hearts of their fathers had been the aim and exultation of his life. They had extended to him an unlimited confidence and an admiration without stint. They had stood by him in the darkest hour, and had borne him from the depths of political despair to the proudest of living positions. Right or wrong, they were men of honour, breeding, and refinement, high and generous character, great weight and station in the country, which they had ever placed at his disposal. They had been not only his followers but his friends; had joined in the same pastimes, drank from the same cup, and in the pleasantness of private life had often forgotten together the cares and strife of politics.

He must have felt something of this, while the Manners, the Somersets, the Bentincks, the Lowthers, and the Lennoxes passed before him. . . .

They trooped on: all the men of metal and large-acred squires, whose spirit he had so often quickened and whose counsel he had so often solicited in his fine conservative speeches in Whitehall Gardens: . . .

The news that the government were not only beaten, but by a majority so large as 73, began to circulate. An incredulous murmur passed it along the treasury bench.

'They say we are beaten by 73!' whispered the most important member of the cabinet in a tone of surprise to Sir Robert Peel.

Sir Robert did not reply or even turn his head. He looked very grave, and extended his chin as was his habit when he was annoyed and cared not to speak. He began to comprehend his position, and that the emperor was without his army.

From Benjamin Disraeli, *Lord George Bentinck* (1852), Constable 1905 ed., pp. 194–6.

Peel resigns

document 23

Four days after the government's defeat Peel delivered his resignation speech, which ended with the following famous peroration.

Sir, I now close the observations which it has been my duty to address to the House, thanking them sincerely for the favour with which they have listened to me in performing this last act of my official career. Within a few hours, probably, that power which I have held for a period of five years will be surrendered into the hands of another — without repining — without complaint on my part — with a more lively recollection of the support and confidence I have received during several years, than of the opposition which during a recent period I have encountered. In relinquishing power, I shall leave a name, severely censured I fear by many who, on public grounds, deeply regret the severance of party ties — deeply regret that severance, not from interested or personal motives, but from the firm conviction that fidelity to party engagements — the existence and maintenance of a great party — constitutes a powerful instrument of government: I shall surrender power severely censured also, by others who, from no interested motive, adhere to the principle of protection, considering the maintenance of it to be essential to the welfare and interests of the country: I shall leave a name execrated by every monopolist who, from less honourable motives, clamours for protection because it conduces to his own individual benefit; but it may be that I shall leave a name sometimes remembered with expressions of good will in the abodes of those whose lot it is to labour, and to earn their daily bread by the sweat of their brow, when they shall recruit their exhausted strength with abundant and untaxed food, the sweeter because it is no longer leavened by a sense of injustice.

Speech in the House of Commons, 29 June 1846, quoted in **11**, iv, pp. 716–17.

The role of party

document 24

The following documents illustrate (a) Peel's disillusionment with the restraints that party loyalty imposes on a Prime Minister; and (b) Disraeli's defence of the claims of party allegiance.

(a) So far from regretting the expulsion from office, I rejoice in it as the greatest relief from an intolerable burden.

To have your own way, and to be for five years the Minister of this country in the House of Commons, is quite enough for any man's strength. He is entitled to his discharge, from length of service. But to have to incur the deepest responsibility, to bear the heaviest toil, to reconcile colleagues with conflicting opinions to a common course of action, to keep together in harmony the Sovereign, the Lords and the Commons; to have to do these things, and to be at the same time the tool of a party — that is to say, to adopt the opinions of men who have not access to your knowledge, and could not profit by it if they had, who spend their time in eating and drinking, and hunting, shooting, gambling, horse-racing, and so forth — would be an odious servitude, to which I never will submit.

I intend to keep aloof from party combinations. So far as a man can be justified in forming such a resolution, I am determined not again to resume office.

I would be nothing but the head of a Government, the real *bona-fide* head, and to be that requires more youth, more ambition, more love of official power and official occupation, than I can pretend to.

I will take care too not again to burn my fingers by organising a party. There is too much truth in the saying, 'The head of a party must be directed by the tail.'

As heads see, and tails are blind, I think heads are the best judges as to the course to be taken.

Peel to Hardinge, 24 September 1846, quoted in **10**, iii, pp. 473–4.

(b) I advise, therefore, that we all — whatever may be our opinions about free trade — oppose the introduction of free politics. Let men stand by the principle by which they rise, right or wrong. I make no exception. If they be in the wrong, they must retire to that shade of private life with which our present rulers have often threatened us. . . . It is not a legitimate trial of the principles of free trade against the principle of protection if a Parliament, the majority of which are elected to support protection, be gained over to free trade by the arts of the very individual whom they were elected to support in an opposite career. It is not fair to the people of England.

Whatever may be the fate of Government: whether we are to have a Whig administration or a Conservative; whether the noble lord or the right hon. gentleman is to wield the sceptre of the state — whatever, I say, may be the fate of Cabinets (and they are transitory and transient things, things which may not survive the career of many men in this House), on Parliament as an institution, and still a popular institution in this country, is dependent, and not upon the Government, the consideration of the vast majority of the members of this House. Do not, then, because you see a great personage giving up his opinions — do not cheer him on, do not give so ready a reward to political tergiversation. Above all, maintain the line of demarcation between parties, for it is only by maintaining the independence of party that you can maintain the integrity of public men, and the power and influence of Parliament itself.

Disraeli, speech in the House of Commons, 22 January 1846, quoted in **88**, ii, pp. 356–7.

document 25

The farmers and repeal

The farmers were particularly active in opposition to any tampering with the Corn Laws; and (as this letter from Innes Lyon, a leading Gloucestershire landowner, to Sir John Fremantle, the Conservative Chief Whip, shows) were more belligerent than many MPs and landowners.

In East Gloucestershire we are peculiarly circumstanced. Both our Conservative Members are, and have been, absent. Lord Bathurst, whom I have seen several times, has been timid to move. Lord Ducie is very active, and decidedly hostile. Lord Fitz Hardinge and the Whigs are for fixed duty – in short, for any measure to embarrass the Government.

It became necessary for some one to move the Farmers – and, *faute de mieux*, I have been actively engaged for the last month in doing so thro' the medium of Peter Mathews, an influential Cotswold Farmer, who looks after my Farms and property there – and himself holds a farm at £1,000 a year.

We are to have a public meeting. They have written to me to propose Resolutions. These can easily be done, but it is wished to go a step further – to present petitions from every Parish against any further alteration of the Corn Laws. Upon this latter point, I wished to have solicited your *personal* advice.

Lyon to Fremantle, January 1844, quoted in **128**, p. 207.

document 26

The death of Peel

The following is typical of many eulogies on Peel after his tragic death on 2 July 1850, especially among the working classes.

He fell from official power into the arms of the people, whose enthusiastic plaudits accompanied him, on the evening of his resignation of office, to his residence in Whitehall Gardens. The spontaneous feeling of gratitude and respect which prompted those plaudits has since widened, strengthened, deepened, and will become more and more vivid and intense as the moral grandeur of his motives – the unselfish, self-sacrificing spirit which dictated his public conduct — pierce through, and consume in the clear and brilliant light of that truth and justice which, we are assured by an illustrious authority, has ever inspired his acts, the calumnious misrepresentations so unsparingly heaped upon him. By his humbler countrymen, that testimony to the moral worth of the departed statesman was not waited for, nor needed. They felt instinctively that he must be pure and single minded, as he was intellectually vigorous and great; for what had he, raised aloft upon the bucklers of a powerful and wealthy party, to gain by stooping from that dazzling height, to raise up the humble and lowly from the mire into which ignorant and partial legislation had so long trampled them.

Obituary article on Sir Robert Peel in Chambers' *Papers for the People*, quoted in **6**, p. 180.

document 27

Gladstone on the Peelites

Gladstone's memorandum, written during Derby's ministry of 1852, indicates the divisions among the Peelites over the problem of their political allegiance.

The truth is these last weeks have been spent in an endeavour to keep the House of Commons together and prevent it coming into a state of crisis by means of a body which does not cohere spontaneously but only holds any kind of unity by constant effort. There are at least four distinct shades among the Peelites. Newcastle stands nearly alone if not quite in the rather high flown idea that we are to create and lead a great virtuous powerful intelligent party, neither the actual Conservative nor the actual Liberal party but a new one. Apart from these witcheries, Graham was ready to take his place in the Liberal ranks; Cardwell Fitzroy and Oswald would I think have gone with him, as F. Peel and Sir C. Douglas went before him. But this section has been arrested, not thoroughly amalgamated, owing to Graham. Thirdly there are the great bulk of the Peelites from Goulburn downwards, more or less undisguisedly anticipating junction with Lord Derby and avowing that free trade is their only point of difference. Lastly, I myself, & I think I am with Lord Aberdeen and S. Herbert, have nearly the same desire, but feel the matter is too crude, & too difficult & important for anticipating any

conclusion, & that our clear line of duty is independence, until the
question of Protection shall be settled.

Gladstone's memorandum, March 1852, quoted in **102**, p. 105.

document 28

Gladstone's Budget, 1853

*Gladstone became Chancellor of the Exchequer in Aberdeen's coalition ministry
of 1852. His Budget of 1853 was a resounding success, and illustrated his
devotion to Peelite principles.*

These little battles were, however, of little moment compared with
the great event of Gladstone's Budget, which came off on Monday
night. He had kept his secret so well, that nobody had the least idea
what it was to be, only it oozed out that the Income Tax was not to
be differentiated. He spoke for five hours, and by universal consent
it was one of the grandest displays and most able financial state-
ments that ever was heard in the H. of Commons; a great scheme,
boldly, skilfully, and honestly devised, disdaining popular clamour
and pressure from without, and the execution of it absolute per-
fection. Even those who do not admire the Budget, or who are injured
by it, admit the merit of the performance. It had raised Gladstone
to a great political elevation, and, what is of far greater consequence than the measure itself, has given the Country assurance
of a *man* equal to great political necessities, and fit to lead parties
and direct Governments.

From *The Greville Memoirs*, 21 April 1853, **12**, vi, pp. 418–19.

document 29

The Aberdeen ministry

*In this extract Greville shrewdly examines the underlying weaknesses of the
Whig-Peelite Coalition government of 1852; weaknesses which helped to bring
about its downfall in 1855.*

The important part of forming the Cabinet is now done, and nothing
remains but the allotment of the places. It will be wonderfully strong
in point of ability, and in this respect exhibit a marked contrast with
the last; but its very excellence in this respect may prove a source
of weakness, and eventually of disunion. The late Cabinet had two

paramount Chiefs, and all the rest nonentities, and the nominal Head was also a real and predominant Head. In the present Cabinet are five or six first-rate men of equal or nearly equal pretensions, none of them likely to acknowledge the superiority or defer to the opinions of any other, and every one of these five or six considering himself abler and more important than their Premier. They are all at present on very good terms and perfectly satisfied with each other; but this satisfaction does not extend beyond the Cabinet itself; murmurings and grumblings are already very loud. The Whigs have never looked with much benignity on this coalition, and they are now furious at the unequal and, as they think, unfair distribution of places that every Peelite should be provided for while half the Whigs or more are left out. These complaints are not without reason, nor will it make matters better that John Russell has had no communication with his old friends and adherents, nor made any struggle (as it is believed) to provide for them, although his adhesion is so indispensable that he might have made any terms and conditions he chose. Thus hampered with difficulties and beset with dangers, it is impossible to feel easy about their prospects. If, however, they set to work vigorously to frame good measures and remove practical and crying evils, they may excite a feeling in their favour in the country, and may attract support enough from different quarters in the H. of Commons to go on, but I much fear that it will at best be a perturbed and doubtful existence.

From *The Greville Memoirs*, 24 December 1852, **12**, v, pp. 384–5.

document 30

The Peelites and Palmerston

Palmerston's resounding victory at the general election of 1857 raised difficult questions for the future of the Peelites, and especially Gladstone, as this letter shows. Sidney Herbert had been Secretary-at-War in Aberdeen's government.

Here, I was, *at the end* of the contest, struck by the fact that *furore* for Palmerston lasted far longer in Conservative than in Liberal households. The regular old-fashioned country gentlemen who are not Londoners enough to have come within the vortex of the Carlton are Palmerstonians *pur et simple*, as the only man who can make peace and ward off democracy. With the Liberals Palmerston is fast becoming secondary to some undefined but not immediate measure of Reform. Indeed, there is a wholesome fear of extreme measures; even those who advocate them hope to be beaten.

As for ourselves – *i.e.* Graham, yourself, and me – we are *rari nantes*, and we are not only broken up as a party (though I maintain we were not one), but the country intends us to be so broken up, and would, I think, resent any attempt at resuscitation. The fear of the cliques and sections is universal, and they bear more than their due in the way of reputation for mischief intended or done. I gather from your Flintshire speeches that you do not consider the result of the elections as a final verdict on past questions, though being engaged in an election, by the way, you, of course, were still pleading the cause.

However, I have written at such length to Lord Aberdeen that I cannot by this post do the same to you. The whole question of our future is very difficult and perplexing, though, within a certain distance, I can see my course ahead clearly enough. I am more puzzled about yours since I read your second letter to Lord Aberdeen, and your difficulties are immediate and not prospective.

Sidney Herbert to Gladstone, 13 April 1857, quoted in **93**, i, pp. 92–3.

Gladstone joins Palmerston

document 31

Despite his earlier antipathy to Palmerston's policies, Gladstone agreed to join his Liberal government in June 1859 for the reasons given below. The formation of this ministry marks in effect the end of the Peelites as a separate group.

When I took my present office in 1859, I had several negative and several positive reasons for accepting it. Of the first, there were these. There had been differences and collisions, but there were no resentments. I felt myself to be mischievous in an isolated position, outside the regular party organization of Parliament. And I was aware of no differences of opinion or tendency likely to disturb the new government. Then on the positive side. I felt sure that in finance there was still much useful work to be done. I was desirous to co-operate in settling the question of the franchise, and failed to anticipate the disaster that it was to undergo. My friends were enlisted, or I knew would enlist: Sir James Graham indeed declining office, but taking his position in the party. And the overwhelming interest and weight of the Italian question, and of our foreign policy in connection with it, joined to my entire mistrust of the former government in relation to it, led me to decide without one moment's hesitation. . . .

Gladstone to Sir John Acton, 1864, quoted **89**, i, p. 628.

Bibliography

PRIMARY SOURCES

1 Aspinall, A., and Smith, E. Anthony, *English Historical Documents 2, 1783–1832*, Eyre and Spottiswoode, 1959.

2 Bamford, Francis, and the Duke of Wellington, *The Journal of Mrs. Arbuthnot*, 2 vols, Macmillan, 1950.

3 Beattie, Alan, ed., *English Party Politics*, 2 vols, vol. I 1600–1906, Weidenfeld and Nicolson, 1970.

4 Brooke, John, and Sorensen, Mary, eds, *The Prime Ministers' Papers: W. E. Gladstone, Autobiographical Memoranda*, 4 vols, vol. II 1832–1845, HMSO, 1972; vol. III 1845–1866, HMSO, 1978; vol. IV 1868–1894, HMSO, 1981.

5 Disraeli, Benjamin, *Coningsby*, Murray, 1844.

6 Gash, Norman, ed., *The Age of Peel* (Documents of Modern History), Arnold, 1968.

7 Jennings, Louis J., ed., *The Croker Papers*, 3 vols, Murray, 1884.

8 Mahon, Lord, and Cardwell, Edward, eds, *Memoirs by Sir Robert Peel*, 2 vols, Murray, 1857.

9 Matthew, H. C. G., ed., *The Gladstone Diaries*, 8 vols, vol. 5 1855–1860; vol. 7 1868–74, Oxford University Press, 1978, 1982.

10 Parker, C. S., ed., *Sir Robert Peel from his Private Papers*, 3 vols, Murray, 1891.

11 *Speeches of Sir Robert Peel*, 4 vols, Murray, 1853.

12 Strachey, Lytton, and Fulford, Roger, eds, *The Greville Memoirs 1814–60*, 8 vols, Macmillan, 1938.

13 Walling, R. A. J., ed., *The Diaries of John Bright*, Cassell, 1930.

SOCIAL AND ECONOMIC BACKGROUND

14 Brown, Lucy, *The Board of Trade and the Free-Trade Movement 1830–42*, Oxford University Press, 1958.

15 Chambers, J. D., and Mingay, G. E., *The Agricultural Revolution*, Batsford, 1966.

16 Crosby, Travis L., *English Farmers and the Politics of Protection*, Harvester Press, 1977.

Bibliography

17 Edsall, Nicholas, *The Anti-Poor Law Movement 1834—41*, Manchester University Press, 1971.

18 Fairlie, S., 'The Nineteenth-Century Corn Law reconsidered', *Economic History Review*, 18, 1965.

19 Lubenow, William C., *The Politics of Government Growth. Early Victorian Attitudes towards State Intervention 1833—1848*, David and Charles, 1971.

20 McCord, Norman, *The Anti-Corn Law League*, Allen and Unwin, 1958.

21 Mathias, Peter, *The First Industrial Nation*, Methuen, 1974 edn.

22 Roberts, David, *Paternalism in Early Victorian England*, Croom Helm, 1979.

23 Ward, J. T., *The Factory Movement 1830—1855*, Macmillan, 1962.

POLITICAL DEVELOPMENT

24 Adelman, Paul, *Victorian Radicalism*, Longman, 1984.

25 Aydelotte, W. O., 'Voting Patterns in the British House of Commons in the 1840s', *Comparative Studies in Sociology and History*, 5, 1963.

26 Aydelotte, W. O., 'Parties and Issues in Early Victorian England', *Journal of British Studies*, 5, 1966.

27 Aydelotte, W. O., 'The Country Gentlemen and the Repeal of the Corn Laws', *English Historical Review*, 82, 1967.

28 Beales, Derek, 'Parliamentary Parties and the 'Independent' Member, 1810—1860', in *Ideas and Institutions of Victorian Britain*, (ed. R. Robson), Bell, 1967.

29 Beales, Derek, *The Parliamentary Parties of Nineteenth-Century Britain*, The Historical Association, 1971.

30 Beckett, J. C., *The Making of Modern Ireland 1603—1923*, Faber, 1969.

31 Bentley, Michael, *Politics without Democracy 1815—1914*, Fontana, 1984.

32 Briggs, Asa, *The Age of Improvement*, Longmans, 1959.

33 Brose, Olive J., *Church and Parliament. The Reshaping of the Church of England 1828—1860*, Stanford University Press, 1959.

34 Cannon, John, *Parliamentary Reform 1640—1832*, Cambridge University Press, 1973.

35 Clark, G. Kitson, 'The Repeal of the Corn Laws and the Politics of the Forties', *Economic History Review*, 4, 1951.

36 Clark, G. Kitson, 'The Electorate and the Repeal of the Corn Laws', *Transactions of the Royal Historical Society*, 1951.

37 Close, David, 'The formation of a two-party alignment in the

House of Commons between 1832 and 1841', *English Historical Review*, 84, 1969.

38   Conacher, J. B., 'Party Politics in the Age of Palmerston', in *1859: Entering an Age of Crisis* (eds Philip Appleman, William Madden, Michael Wolff), Indiana University Press, 1959.

39   Conacher, J. B., *The Aberdeen Coalition 1852–1855*, Cambridge University Press, 1968.

40   Evans, Eric J., *The Forming of the Modern State. Early Industrial Britain 1783–1870*, Longman, 1983.

41   Evans, Eric J., *Political Parties in Britain 1783–1867* (Lancaster Pamphlets), Methuen, 1985.

42   Foord, A. S., 'The Waning of the Influence of the Crown', *English Historical Review*, 62, 1947.

43   Foord, A. S., *His Majesty's Opposition 1714–1830*, Oxford University Press, 1964.

44   Gash, Norman, *Politics in the Age of Peel*, Longmans, 1953.

45   Gash, Norman, *Reaction and Reconstruction in English Politics 1832–1852*, Oxford University Press, 1965.

46   Gash, Norman, *Aristocracy and People. Britain 1815–1865*, Arnold, 1979.

47   Gurowich, P. M., 'The Continuation of War by Other Means: Party and Politics, 1855–1865', *The Historical Journal*, 27, 1984.

48   Harvey, A. D., *Britain in the Early Nineteenth Century*, Batsford, 1978.

49   Hill, B. W., *British Parliamentary Parties 1742–1832*, Allen and Unwin, 1985.

50   Johnson, D. W. J., 'Sir James Graham and the "Derby Dilly" ', *Birmingham Historical Journal*, 4, 1953–54.

51   Kemp, Betty, 'The General Election of 1841', *History*, 37, 1952.

52   Kemp, Betty, 'Reflections on the Repeal of the Corn Laws', *Victorian Studies*, 5, 1961–62.

53   Large, David, 'The House of Lords and Ireland in the age of Peel, 1832–50', *Irish Historical Studies*, 9, 1955.

54   Lawson-Tancred, Mary, 'The Anti-League and the Corn Law Crisis of 1846', *The Historical Journal*, 3, 1960.

55   Machin, G. I. T., *The Catholic Question in English Politics 1820 to 1830*, Oxford University Press, 1964.

56   Machin, G. I. T., *Politics and the Churches in Great Britain 1832 to 1868*, Oxford University Press, 1977.

57   Macdonagh, Oliver, 'O'Connell and Repeal, 1840–45', in *High*

Bibliography

and Low Politics in Modern Britain (eds Michael Bentley and John Stevenson), Oxford University Press, 1983.

58 McDowell, R. B., *Public Opinion and Government Policy in Ireland, 1801—1846*, Faber, 1952.

59 Macintyre, Angus, *The Liberator. Daniel O'Connell and the Irish Party 1830—1847*, Hamish Hamilton, 1965.

60 Martin, Kingsley, *The Triumph of Lord Palmerston*, Hutchinson, 1963 edn.

61 Mather, F. C., *Public Order in the Age of the Chartists*, Manchester University Press, 1959.

62 Mather, F. C., 'The Government and the Chartists', in *Chartist Studies* (ed. Asa Briggs), Macmillan, 1965.

63 Mitchell, Austin, *The Whigs in Opposition 1815—30*, Oxford University Press, 1967.

64 Mosse, George L., 'The Anti-League: 1844—1846', *Economic History Review*, 17—18, 1947—48.

65 Namier, Lewis, *Monarchy and the Party System*, Oxford University Press, 1952.

66 Norman, E. R., *Anti-Catholicism in Victorian England*, Allen and Unwin, 1968.

67 Norman, E. R., *Church and Society in England 1770—1970*, Oxford University Press, 1976.

68 Nowlan, Kevin B., *The Politics of Repeal. A Study in the Relations between Great Britain and Ireland, 1841—50*, Routledge, 1965.

69 O'Gorman, Frank, *The Emergence of the British Two-Party System*, Arnold, 1982.

70 Pares, Richard, *King George III and the Politicians*, Oxford University Press, 1953.

71 Royle, Edward, *Chartism*, Longman, 1980.

72 Stuart, C. H. 'The Formation of the Coalition Cabinet of 1852', *Transactions of the Royal Historical Society*, 1954.

73 Vincent, J. R. 'The Parliamentary Dimensions of the Crimean War', *Transactions of the Royal Historical Society*, 31, 1981.

BIOGRAPHIES

74 Blake, Robert, *Disraeli*, Eyre and Spottiswoode, 1966; University Paperbacks, 1969.

75 Chamberlain, Muriel E., *Lord Aberdeen*, Longman, 1983.

76 Clark, G. Kitson, *Peel*, Duckworth, 1936.

77 Disraeli, Benjamin, *Lord George Bentinck* (1852), Constable 1905 edn.

78 Driver, C. R., *Tory Radical. The Life of Richard Oastler*, Oxford University Press, 1946.

79 Finlayson, Geoffrey B. A. M., *The Seventh Earl of Shaftesbury 1801–1885*, Eyre Methuen, 1981.

80 Gash, Norman, *Mr. Secretary Peel*, Longmans, 1961; 2nd edn. 1985.

81 Gash, Norman, *Sir Robert Peel. The Life of Sir Robert Peel after 1830*, Longman, 1972; 2nd edn. 1986.

82 Gash, Norman, *Peel*, Longman, 1977: an abridgement of **80** and **81**.

83 Gash, Norman, 'The Earl of Liverpool' in *The Prime Ministers*, vol. 1 (ed. Herbert Van Thal), Allen and Unwin, 1974.

84 Gash, Norman, *Lord Liverpool*, Weidenfeld and Nicolson, 1984.

85 Hodder, Edwin, *Life and Work of the Seventh Earl of Shaftesbury*, 3 vols, Cassell, 1886.

86 Longford, Elizabeth, *Wellington. Pillar of State*, Weidenfeld and Nicolson, 1972.

87 Matthew, H. C. G., *Gladstone 1809–1874*, Oxford University Press, 1986.

88 Monepenny, W. F., and Buckle, G. E., *The Life of Benjamin Disraeli, Earl of Beaconsfield*, vols 1–4, Murray, 1910–16.

89 Morley, John, *The Life of Gladstone*, Macmillan, 2 vol. edn, 1905.

90 Parker, C. S., *Life and Letters of Sir James Graham*, 2 vols, Murray, 1907.

91 Ramsay, A. A. W., *Sir Robert Peel*, Constable, 1928.

92 Shannon, Richard, *Gladstone*, vol. i, Hamish Hamilton, 1982; University Paperback, 1984.

93 Stanmore, Lord, *Sidney Herbert. A Memoir*, 2 vols, Murray, 1906.

94 Ward, J. T., *Sir James Graham*, Macmillan, 1967.

95 Whibley, Charles, *Lord John Manners and his Friends*, 2 vols, Blackwood, 1925.

96 Yonge, C. D., *The Life of Robert Banks, Second Earl of Liverpool*, 3 vols, Macmillan, 1868.

THE CONSERVATIVE PARTY

97 Blake, Robert, *The Conservative Party from Peel to Thatcher*, Fontana Press, 1985.

98 Bradfield, B. T., 'Sir Richard Vyvyan and the Country Gentlemen, 1830–1834', *English Historical Review*, 83, 1968.

99 Brock, W. R., *Lord Liverpool and Liberal Toryism 1820–1827*, Cambridge University Press, 1941; Cass edn., 1967.

100 Clark, G. Kitson, *Peel and the Conservative Party. A Study in Party Politics 1832–1841*, Bell, 1929; Cass edn., 1964.

101 Conacher, J. B., 'Peel and the Peelites, 1846–1850', *English Historical Review*, 73, 1958.

102 Conacher, J. B., *The Peelites and the Party System 1846–52*, David and Charles, 1972.

103 Cookson, J. E., *Lord Liverpool's Administration. The Crucial Years 1815–1822*, Scottish Academic Press, 1975.

104 Crosby, Travis L., *Sir Robert Peel's Administration 1841–1846*, David and Charles, 1976.

105 Davis, Richard W., 'Toryism to Tamworth: The Triumph of Reform, 1827–1835', *Albion*, 12, 1980.

106 Donajgrodzki, A. P., 'Sir James Graham at the Home Office', *The Historical Journal*, 20, 1977.

107 Faber, Richard, *Young England*, Faber, 1987.

108 Fisher, D. R., 'Peel and the Conservative Party. The Sugar Crisis of 1844 Reconsidered', *The Historical Journal*, 18, 1975.

109 Gash, Norman, 'Ashley and the Conservative Party in 1842', *English Historical Review*, 53, 1938.

110 Gash, Norman, 'Peel and the Party System 1830–50', *Transactions of the Royal Historical Society*, 5th series, vol. 1, 1951.

111 Gash, Norman, 'F. R. Bonham: Conservative "Political Secretary", 1832–47', *English Historical Review*, 63, 1948.

112 Gash, Norman, 'Wellington and Peel', in *The Conservative Leadership 1832–1932*, ed. Donald Southgate, Macmillan, 1974.

113 Gash, Norman, 'From the Origins to Sir Robert Peel', in *The Conservatives*, (ed. Lord Butler), Allen and Unwin, 1977.

114 Gash, Norman, 'The Historical Significance of the Tamworth Manifesto', in *Pillars of Government*, Arnold, 1986.

115 Gash, Norman, 'The Founder of Modern Conservatism', in *Pillars of Government*, Arnold, 1986.

116 Hill, R. L., *Toryism and the People 1832–1846*, Constable, 1929.

117 Hilton, Boyd, *Corn, Cash, Commerce. The Economic Policies of the Tory Governments 1815–1830*, Oxford University Press, 1977.

118 Hilton, Boyd, 'Peel: A Reappraisal', *The Historical Journal*, 22, 1979.

119 Jones, W. D., *Lord Derby and Victorian Conservatism*, Blackwell, 1956.

120 Jones, W. D., and Erickson, A. B., *The Peelites 1846–1857*, Ohio State University Press, 1972.

121 Kerr, Donal A., *Peel, Priests and Politics*, Oxford University Press, 1982.

122 Newbould, Ian, 'Sir Robert Peel and the Conservative party, 1832–1841: A study in failure?', *English Historical Review*, 98, 1983.

123 Read, Donald, *Peel and the Victorians*, Blackwell, 1987.

124 Roberts, David, 'Tory Paternalism and Social Reform in Early Victorian England', *American Historical Review*, 63, 1958.

125 Smith, Paul, *Disraelian Conservatism and Social Reform*, Routledge, 1967.

126 Stewart, Robert, 'The Ten Hours and Sugar Crises of 1844: Government and the House of Commons in the Age of Reform', *The Historical Journal*, 12, 1969.

127 Stewart, Robert, *The Politics of Protection. Lord Derby and the Protectionist Party 1841–1852*, Cambridge University Press, 1971.

128 Stewart, Robert, *The Foundation of the Conservative Party 1830–1867*, Longman, 1978.

129 Welch, P. J., 'Blomfield and Peel: a Study in Co-operation between Church and State, 1841–46', *Journal of Ecclesiastical History*, 12, 1961.

130 Clark, G. Kitson, 'Hunger and Politics in 1842', *Journal of Modern History*, 25, 1953.

Index